Journey for Justice

Journey for Justice

The Life and Work of Rev. Fr. Michael Rodrigo, OMI: Interfaith Dialogue in Action for Empowering the Rural Poor of Sri Lanka

NANDINI GUNEWARDENA

Foreword by Aloysius Pieris, SJ

WIPF & STOCK · Eugene, Oregon

JOURNEY FOR JUSTICE
The Life and Work of Rev. Fr. Michael Rodrigo, OMI: Interfaith Dialogue in Action for Empowering the Rural Poor of Sri Lanka

Copyright © 2017 Nandini Gunewardena. All rights reserved. Except for brief quotations in critical publications or reviews, no part of this book may be reproduced in any manner without prior written permission from the publisher. Write: Permissions, Wipf and Stock Publishers, 199 W. 8th Ave., Suite 3, Eugene, OR 97401.

Wipf & Stock
An Imprint of Wipf and Stock Publishers
199 W. 8th Ave., Suite 3
Eugene, OR 97401

www.wipfandstock.com

PAPERBACK ISBN: 978-1-5326-0779-0
HARDCOVER ISBN: 978-1-5326-0781-3
EBOOK ISBN: 978-1-5326-0780-6

Manufactured in the U.S.A.   MAY 17, 2017

Contents

Foreword by Aloysius Pieris, SJ | *vii*
Acknowledgments | *xi*
Abbreviations | *xv*
Introduction | *xvii*

1. Early Life: The Journey Begins | 1
2. Engagements in Faith: Liturgical Leader, Teacher, and Social Justice Activist | 20
3. Bridge of Faith: Dialogue, Dialogy, and Key Theological Perspectives | 34
4. Faith for Justice: Life and Mission of Suba-Seth Gedera | 52
5. Transformational Faith: Embracing Death for Justice | 83
6. Epilogue—Aftermath: The Voice Not Silenced | 96

Appendix: Testimonials | *119*
Bibliography | *127*

Foreword

Rev. Fr. Aloysius Pieris, SJ

When I think of Fr. Michael Rodrigo—my senior in the presbyterate and religious life, but a friend and colleague in the mission of inter-religious dialogue and social justice—I cannot help recalling St. Paul's message to the Philippians about Jesus. Often mistranslated as "although in the form of God" he humbled himself (insinuating that it is uncharacteristic of God to be humble) the Greek text clearly states, "Being [*huparchōn*] in the form of God," i.e., *because* he was divine he "did not cling" (*ouk harpagmon*) to his being equal to God but emptied himself of his divinity (*ekenosen*) by taking the human form; and even as a human he opted to descend to a lower social level (*etapeinosen*) so that finally he was brutally murdered in the humiliating manner reserved only for criminal slaves, the scum of the Roman society . . . only to be raised to glory.

Michael was a true follower of his meek and humble Master. "Not clinging" (*ouk harpagmon*) to his prestige in the academe or his family status, he climbed down the social ladder (*etapeinosen*) to share the life-struggle of the politically victimized and economically exploited peasants and paid a heavy price for it with his precious life . . . "having become obedient unto death" (*genomenos hupēkoos mechri thanatou*); but God "exalted him" (*huperupsōsen*) as a martyr to justice, inspiring a number of clerical and lay groups to start new gospel-based movements for ensuring religious harmony and social justice. He did not die in vain.

Some church leaders did refuse to recognize him as a martyr; they referred to him—in private conversation of course—as a victim of his own political naïveté and infantile adventurism. It is not surprising, however, that such an unfair verdict could come from the members of the Catholic elite, both lay and clerical, since they were overtly supportive of the governing party that eliminated Michael. It was this very government that introduced a presidential dictatorship in 1978 and connived in its own party-members unleashing an anti-minority pogrom in 1983, which precipitated a disastrous interethnic war. Any wonder that those supportive of the political system which targeted Michael as a political threat found it embarrassing to recognize his assassination as the price he paid for witnessing to Christ among the marginalized in the rural South? On the other hand, the suffering masses in the farming community and their frustrated youth—almost all non-Christian—saw in him a gentle and humble recluse who nevertheless dared to risk his life by accompanying them in their search for survival and safety.

From the fruits you shall know. It was not only the Buddhists in the South that revered him as one who died on their behalf, but many Catholic seminarians of the time believed that they too were beneficiaries of his martyrdom; for they were so vehement in repudiating the clericalism, which Michael's life and death critiqued, that they banded themselves together to form a group that would perpetuate in their lives the new model of ministerial priesthood and which their hero's life and death had revealed. This movement, growing ever stronger, is known as Kitusara (The Arrow of Christ) and is being supported and joined by an increasing number of young laypersons. The latest news is that on the fourth of March this year (2016) this movement has launched their trilingual website www.jesustodaysl.org.

Michael did not die in vain. As all martyrs do, he has allowed the manner of his death to project a large picture of his life that was until then hidden from the rest of the country and which was marked by a fearless fidelity to the gospel.

Let me conclude this foreword with a personal note. Michael was a trusted friend of mine. During many of his visits to Colombo, he would end his eight-hour journey at our Tulana Centre located in a suburb of the metropolis. Next morning he would leave for the city without breakfast. His overnight sojourn with us was a treat that we always waited for. Supper and witty conversations spiced with puns were part of what we always enjoyed during his visits. Yet, it was his experiences at Buttala, narrated tersely but touchingly, that were spiritually stirring and theologically stimulating. At

Foreword

each visit, he left behind a word or two that the Lord had spoken to him through the rural poor in the deep-South. I began to hear them clearly only after the assassin's bullet had pierced his head, shattered his brain, and filled the chalice with his blood; when the Last Supper of the Lord, which he was celebrating, climaxed in his brutal death, as in the case of his master. Yes, very much like his master! For he *has risen* in the hearts of so many that no one can muffle his voice now. This book is an instance of it. I am grateful to the authoress for having allowed me to add my mite to it.

Acknowledgments

GIVEN THE IMMENSE SPIRITUAL and social significance of Father Michael Paul Rodrigo, OMI (1927–1987), whose life trajectory this biography focuses on, the author made a conscious effort to seek recollections from a broad swath of individuals who were acquainted with him in some capacity or the other across his life. The author sincerely acknowledges each of their contributions to this volume with deep appreciation.

This volume was launched based on a consensus reached with Fr. Mike's surviving family members (his nieces and nephews), who enthusiastically agreed to the idea of the biography and who extended their generous support in terms of time and energy in many ways. They provided initial feedback on the proposed structure of the book, connected the author with leading representatives of the Oblate community in Sri Lanka and other key individuals who had known Fr. Mike (i.e., his surviving relatives, colleagues, acquaintances, and students), assembled and shared various material the family had collected over the years about Fr. Mike (personal letters, newspaper articles, and other documents), and took time to review numerous drafts of the manuscript. The author expresses her deep gratitude to each of them. Mrs. Devayani (Devi) Solomons (née Rodrigo, Fr. Mike's elder brother Sam's daughter) was the first contact. Her warm and prayerful encouragement for this project from the start moved it forward. She connected the author with her siblings and cousins and provided key clarifications along the way. Richard Rodrigo (Sam's son, and Devi's elder brother) assumed a vital role in connecting the author with the community of Oblate priests and other religious figures and scholars who had either known or were familiar with Fr. Mike's mission. The logistical arrangements

Acknowledgments

he made for meetings with these individuals were a tremendous asset in this endeavor. Algernon (Algi) Wijewickrema (Fr. Mike's elder sister Petronella's son) proved to be a valuable source of background information and family history. Shantini De Silva (née Rodrigo, Sam's eldest daughter and Devi's older sister) willingly shared a volume of personal documents and warm memories, while continuing to encourage the author with prayers. Eulalie (Eula, Petronella's daughter) also shared letters that Fr. Mike had written as well as heartwarming memories. Michael Rodrigo (Sam's eldest son) recounted stories of his "escapades" with Fr. Mike and served as an inspiration in upholding the values and struggles for justice true to Fr. Mike's legacy. Other family members who supported this project in numerous ways through snippets of their memories, paper cuttings, photos and other mementos, helpful suggestions, and caring words include Priyanthi (Sam's youngest daughter) and her husband Lukshman, Dushyanthi (Richard's wife), Shanthi (Algi's wife), Ranjit (Shantini's husband), Maxwell (Devi's husband), and Mrs. Hiranthi Fernando (Fr. Mike's cousin's daughter). Fr. Mike's cousin, Mr. Merrill Fernando, is gratefully acknowledged for his generous contribution to support this publication as well the fond remembrances he provided.

Heartfelt thanks also go to several leading members of the Oblate community for the invaluable time they devoted to sharing their recollections of Fr. Mike with the author and for the clarifications on various aspects of his theological perspectives, his commitments, and his vision. Fr. Rohan Silva, OMI, Oblate provincial director whose commendable leadership and support to sustain Fr. Mike's legacy instilled this volume with credence. Fr. Claude Perera, OMI, chaplain superior at Peradeniya University, Sri Lanka, was one of the first individuals with whom the author broached the idea of this endeavor. He served as an excellent source of contextual information, theological and conceptual clarifications, and much encouragement throughout. Fr. Oswald Firth, OMI, who remembers Fr. Mike as his first teacher at the seminary provided key background details on the events and processes that inspired and fired Fr. Mike's theological developments. Fr. Romesh Lowe, OMI, liturgical instructor, Ampitiya National Seminary, shared valuable interpretations on complex liturgical concepts that Fr. Mike had advanced (including Fr. Mike's concept of Passover), which was incorporated into his doctoral thesis and proposed as a relevant theology for the local church. Fr. Bonnie Fernandopulle, a former student of Fr. Mike, parish priest, St. Mary's Church Dehiwela, and Episcopal vicar for the

ACKNOWLEDGMENTS

Western Region of the Archdiocese of Colombo, shared his impressions of Fr. Mike's unique gifts and quest. Fr. Clement Waidyasekara took time out of his busy schedule to locate key archival documents, including Fr. Mike's doctoral thesis at the Gregorian Institute of Rome and made connections to key resource persons. The Very Rev. Fr. Mervyn Fernando, PhD, founder and President of the Subodhi Institute for Integral Education and Mr. Ray Forbes, brother of Fr. Mike's dear friend the late Rev. Dalston Forbes, OMI, kindly shared some important recollections. Br. Rabindra Rajapakse, OMI, who has been steadfastly continuing the work at Suba Seth Gedera since 2013 accommodated the author with kindness and generosity during her research visit in July 2016 and provided important updates on the situation in the village area. The steadfast dedication of Mr. Louis Benedict to finding justice for Fr. Mike and the eloquent elucidation of his ideas by Prof. Anton Meemane have been founts of illumination in this endeavor. The long-term efforts of Sr. Milburga Fernando in documenting and publishing Fr. Mike's thoughts and commitments have made an inestimable contribution to this biography. The author is especially grateful to her and to Sr. Benedict Fernandopulle for the many lengthy conversations which yielded much needed detail on their work with Fr. Mike at Suba Seth Gedera, as well as for the precious memories of the author's time there in 1987. Sr. Winifreda Wasalathanthrige shared several recollections of her acquaintance of Fr. Mike that were immensely useful in filling in the information gaps. The author is grateful for her caring correspondence, even in the midst of her challenging work on prison outreach to women in Uganda. The good wishes and prayers of all these individuals sustained the author during the isolated long days of drafting this manuscript.

Of utmost value to this project is the heartfelt endorsement by Fr. Aloysius Pieris, SJ (founder and director of Tulana Research Centre for Encounter and Dialogue in Kelaniya, Sri Lanka), Fr. Mike's long-time friend and colleague. He was a source of steady encouragement to the author, while his sagacious guidance at critical junctures of this project helped steer its course. He generously provided inimitable insights on Fr. Mike's spiritual quest, his profound theological concepts, and shed light on the many challenges of the day that Fr. Mike had grappled with. His Eminence, Cardinal Malcolm Ranjith, Archbishop of Colombo, graciously extended time to meet the author and provide warm recollections of his time as Fr. Mike's student, including key aspects of his theological orientations.

Acknowledgments

Several other individuals extended their support for this endeavor in varying ways, through prayers, words of encouragement, and kind deeds that allowed the author to make steady progress on the volume. At the outset, upon hearing of the author's intention to undertake this biography, Kristie Paylor took it upon herself to research publications referencing Fr. Mike's work. Ms. Paylor also offered to take care of the author's two children while she traveled to Sri Lanka in July 2016 to collect the material and conduct the interviews for this volume. Ashley Dias made regular check-ins to reinforce the importance of this volume and provide snippets from his acquaintance with Fr. Mike during his time at the seminary. Reginald De Silva, a youngster during Fr. Mike's time as the Boys Town mayor, also filled in details about vital place markers in Fr. Mike's life, including Dehiwela, St. Mary's Church, the novitiate house, and the Borella seminary. His vivid recollections, narrated humorously, provided the author a good sense of the social climate of the Catholic community in Dehiwela. Affectionate acknowledgement is made of his daughter, Sr. Swedini Halliday (née De Silva), whose enduring friendship with Devi Solomons made the initial connection that enabled the author to embark on this volume. Last but not least, to all the villagers at Alukalavita who provided their sincere and heartrending testimonials, the author expresses her sincere thanks. More than anything, their impressions provided insight into Fr. Mike's love for the *ochlos*, God's chosen people, to whom he witnessed Jesus. Any shortcomings are attributable to the author. Sincere thanks to Brian Palmer of Wipf & Stock publishers for seeing early on the potential of this book, and to all the staff who played key roles during the publication process: Matthew Wimer, Chelsea Lobey and Jana.

Abbreviations

AHRC—Asian Human Rights Commission
CSR—Center for Society and Religion
COIN—counter-insurgency campaign
GCE—General Certificate of Education
ILO—International Labor Organization
JVP—Janatha Vimukthi Peramuna
OMI—Oblates of Mary Immaculate
PD—Participatory Development
PSC—Pelwatte Sugar Corporation
SDS—Sisters of the Divine Savior
SJ—Society of Jesus
SSG—Suba Seth Gedera
WMV—Waguruwela Maha Vidyalaya

Introduction

> "Everyone who struggles for justice, everyone who makes just claims in unjust surroundings, is working for God's reign even though not a Christian. The church does not comprise all of God's reign; God's reign goes beyond church boundaries."
>
> —Oscar Romero, Bishop, Cardinal, El Salvador.

AUTHOR'S REFLECTIONS

EACH NOVEMBER, AS THE leaves turn color from the green of summer to the gold and orange hues of autumn in the Western regions of the world, we have pause for reflection on the eternal cycle of transitions and how God infuses beauty even in the midst of loss and grief. In much of Sri Lanka, November is the month for the incessant Northeastern monsoon rains. It is also the month for Deepavali, the Hindu festival of lights that signifies the victory of good over evil. For the Buddhists of Sri Lanka, the November (*il masa*) full moon (*Poya*) is the penultimate *Poya* of the annual calendar because it is the last one of the rainy season, when several events key to the Buddhist calendar took place: the announcement of the future attainment of Buddhahood by Gautama Buddha, the initiation of Buddhist missionary activity by sixty arahats (deeply spiritual individuals committed to the Buddhist spiritual path), the festival of Devahaona (ascendency to heaven by the Buddha), the acceptance of a robe from the future Buddha-to-be from a disciple (a signal of the complete renunciation of life and full commitment to the spiritual journey), and the passing away of Dharmasenapathi, one of the Buddha's chief disciples, Venerable Sariputta.

As each November approaches, I am left recalling that heart-wrenching phone call at 5 a.m. on November 11, 1987, with the news that Fr. Michael

Introduction

Rodrigo, OMI, beloved spiritual mentor and intellectual guide had been fatally shot the previous night at his residence, Suba Seth Gedera, in Alukalavita village, Buttala, Sri Lanka (see map, p. 5). As the floor beneath me seemed to slip away, the mere thought of this loss and the motive behind his demise was unfathomable. How could such an illuminating spiritual force who worked tirelessly for decades on behalf of the impoverished of Lanka be blighted so swiftly? Even thirty years hence, that is still perplexing to me and to scores of others who were touched by his work and words in some way or another.

Fr. Mike has been acclaimed a prophet for the cause of peace, a pacifist priest deeply devoted to Jesus Christ while embracing ecumenism and interfaith dialogue, a liturgical leader with penetrating insights fulfilled through praxis, an anti-poverty activist with the unflinching endurance of a martyr, and an incisive intellectual, gifted with a poetic vision. His sacrifice of self for the cause of justice for the poor and the oppressed has spurred and inspired generations of justice workers in the faith community and the laity alike. In a world where examples abound of Christians who strive to emulate and carry on Jesus Christ's mission for humanity, Fr. Mike stands out as an exceptional soul who unreservedly lived out Christ's summons to humanity of compassion and caritas. Far more than a foot soldier working in the trenches against poverty, social discrimination, and economic injustice, he exemplified a divinely guided spiritual direction in speaking out against injustice. He faced physical hardship and political challenges with indomitable courage, and tirelessly endured trials of many sorts along his life journey for justice.

The story of Fr. Mike, his courage, his brilliant scholarship, his sharp wit, his poetic words, his immeasurable compassion and self-sacrifice has been recounted by many before me. To them, we owe a world of thanks for ensuring that his message, his theology, his undeterred commitment to empowering the poor, his vision of the essential call of Christian life—to serve the poor—has not been forgotten. Among them are leading Christian theologians and scholars such as Rev. Fr. Aloysius Pieris, SJ, PhD (Tulana Institute, Sri Lanka), Prof. Anton Meemana, PhD (Aquinas University, Sri Lanka), and Rev. Fr. Claude Perera, OMI, PhD (Peradeniya University, Sri Lanka). Sr. Milburga Fernando who lived and worked with him at Suba Seth Gedera has been at the forefront of several publications that have made it possible for the public at large to gain a broader understanding of Fr. Mike's thought and vision. Several younger scholars have also analyzed

Introduction

his ideas and the meaning of his life and untimely death.[1] Thus, his legacy is alive, thriving, and inspirational beyond the sixty years of his physical existence and the thirty years hence.

This biography traces Fr. Mike's passage through life, in an attempt to chronicle his spiritual evolution from an early age through to the complex theological advances that guided his quest for interfaith understanding, across a life passage that can only be summed up as a journey for social justice. A valiant champion of social and economic equity, Fr. Mike exemplified the epitome of self-sacrifice in his commitment to ushering justice for the poor. He was resolute to the end in his refusal to abandon his commitment to the poor, especially of Buttala, which had been reduced to poverty as a result of centuries of deliberate acts that undermined its livelihood security. These acts included the wanton disruption of the primary source of livelihood security for the rice farming communities of Buttala—the destruction of the network of water reservoirs that nurtured the agricultural system by British colonial forces in their attempt to quell the peasant uprising of 1818. Subsequent decades of neglect in the aftermath of independence, and recent development strategies that entailed dispossession, displacement, and corporate exploitation (e.g., land expropriation for the Pelwatte Sugar Corporation) further complicate their indigence. A pacifist at heart, Fr. Mike responded with immense acts of compassion to restore their dignity, regain their human rights, resuscitate their self-reliance, and reduce their vulnerability. Almost singularly, yet through collaborative, participatory approaches designed for their self-determination, he worked tirelessly *with* the poor for the intertwined aims of social and economic empowerment. This book is a tribute to that dauntless journey for justice.

Fr. Mike chose the Uva region of Southeastern Sri Lanka for his vision of realizing social justice expressly for the purpose of redressing the long record of outright violations against the religious, social, cultural, and economic sovereignty of the population. Given the harsh terrain and inhospitable eco-climatic conditions of the region, his physical shift alone to the region known as Lower Uva represented an enormous self-sacrifice. It is, however, the attendant spiritual transformations which grounded and inspired his quest that makes his life extraordinary and his journey for justice exemplary. It was indeed a selfless journey for justice, even as his life was threatened, to the point of sacrificing his life on behalf of the poor. The grave injustice of his assassination leaves us questioning fundamental

1. Lowe, "Word-Crucified."

Introduction

aspects of the social fabric of the country that would allow such acts of inhumanity. These are issues central for understanding contemporary Sri Lankan society, its political processes, systems, and economic structures. In the end, the Christian values of nonviolence, compassion, and kindness that Fr. Mike advocated, his elucidation of their parallels in Buddhism— *Ahimsa, metta, karuna*—offer hope for a resolute path ahead for achieving national peace and reconciliation. While his exemplary life trajectory is inspirational enough, his visionary efforts in building a bridge of understanding across the diverse communities of Sri Lanka offer a plausible model for future steps in national healing, inclusivity, tolerance, and coexistence.

Fr. Mike's courage to speak up on behalf of the poor and confront the forces of oppression left an indelible mark on many young people. I am one of those whose life has been irrevocably touched by his engagement with social and economic justice and his spiritual vision. Fr. Mike was killed because he was a revolutionary, not in the sense of a militant—no, his approach was not one of terror tactics—yet he can be considered a freedom fighter because he fought against oppression both spiritual and material. He strove for freedom of the spirit, freedom from hunger, freedom from domination by oppressive forces. He did not resort to arms—he was an apostle of peace, a mild mannered man with a sharp tongue and gentle voice, a critical thinker who dared to venture beyond the safety of the ivory tower cloisters and live amongst the poorest of poor peasants in the most developmentally marginalized area of the county, Moneragala District. Thus the irony of his death at the hands of an assassin who gunned him down from the back in a cowardly, cold-blooded gesture of violence. The assassin had aimed for his head—symbolizing the threat that Fr. Mike's unconventional ideas about equity and social justice represented to the conservative political forces of the time. With his death, Sri Lanka suffered a deeper loss than we realize. Fr. Mike embodied a ray of hope for the future, for an autonomous, harmonious nation.

Like myself, countless others have resolved to emulate his commitment to serve the poor and to find redress for their disenfranchisement. His wholehearted embrace of the impoverished youth of Lanka in their own (perhaps misguided) attempts to rectify the oppressive conditions of their existence has paved a way to their acknowledgement of Christ in his redemptive role. And that perhaps was Fr. Mike's ultimate purpose—to witness Christ to the poor, to the Buddhist poor of Lower Uva, in a way that heralds the cosmic nature of Christ in restoring the harmonious balance of

Introduction

the universe. The virtues of sacrifice and compassion that he exemplified, infused with that warm smile, understanding nod, friendly repartee, and witty response, transformed the lives of those he touched. The author hopes that the ensuing account of Fr. Mike's journey for justice will deepen the resolve of many a reader to carry out Christ's summons to each of us.

1

Early Life
The Journey Begins[1]

THE REMARKABLE JOURNEY OF faith undertaken by the exemplary human being affectionately referred to as Father (Fr.) Mike begins on June 30, 1927 in the small suburb of Dehiwela, approximately twelve kilometers south of Colombo (then capital city of the island nation of Sri Lanka).[2] Born in to a devout Catholic family, Sinhasunkage[3] Michael Paul Rodrigo was the youngest of six children (all deceased now), in descending order: Hilda, Petronella, Samuel, Beatrice, and Gertride. Hailing initially from the southern town of Galle (see map, p. 5), his parents, Sinhasunkage Richard

---

1. The biographical details in this chapter are derived from personal interviews undertaken by the author with family members and friends well acquainted with Fr. Mike, printed versions of his own thoughts, as well as online commentaries by various authors.

2. At the time, the country was a part of the British Commonwealth and called Ceylon even after gaining independence in 1948. In 1972, upon becoming a republic, a decision was made to revert to its original name Lanka, with the honorific "Sri" attached to signify "resplendent" island. Although Colombo is still recognized as the nation's geographic center, the seat of government was moved in 1990 to a location eight kilometers east, to the ancient city of Kotte, by then renamed Sri Jayawardenapura.

3. According to customary practices among the Sinhala population of Sri Lanka, the family name (*vasagama*) is usually placed first, and denoted the name of the lineage, and/or service performed in the past under the royal system (*rajakariya*). Typically, the family name also included the name of the village where the person's ancestors had resided or originated from. Although the use of the *ge* name (as the latter is referred to) has virtually disappeared in contemporary practice, Fr. Mike was baptized inclusive of the *ge* name Sinhasunkage, which is also engraved on his grave stone. It is included here upon the request of his surviving family members, but omitted in the rest of the manuscript, given that he rarely used it during his lifetime.

Alexander Rodrigo and Georgiana Rodrigo (née Panambarage) had settled in Dehiwela in the early 1900s, at a time when Sri Lanka was still under British rule. Theirs was a middle-class family intensely steeped in spiritual practice, not only within the home but also beyond, in charitable causes, and faith activities in their home parish, St. Mary's Church, Dehiwela. It was customary practice for the Rodrigo family (as with most Sri Lankan Catholics) to light an oil lamp each night, symbolic of Jesus as the light of the world, recite the rosary together, and join in a common prayer prior to retiring. They were a close-knit family, which undoubtedly created a devout and nurturing milieu for young Michael's faith journey. From all available accounts, it is clear that his immediate and extended family had laid the early foundations that cultivated Fr. Mike's spiritual formation.

This chapter traces some of the early influences that facilitated the personal and spiritual transformations and shaped the theological insights, vision, and commitments of Fr. Mike, the incomparable priest, scholar, poet, activist, and martyr for the cause of social justice. The background information contained in this chapter can be credited to generous sharing of personal anecdotes, letters, and other information by Fr. Mike's surviving nine nieces and nephews: Shantini, Michael, Richard, Devayani and Priyanthi (Sam's children), and Eulalie, Marie, Algernon, and Aloy (Petronella's children).

EARLY LIFE

A JOURNEY PREDESTINED?

Given the middle name Paul in honor of St. Paul, whose feast falls on June 29, the day before he was born, Fr. Mike's life journey embodies some uncanny parallels to the physical and spiritual courses traversed by Paul, the apostle. St. Paul is considered one of the most important figures in the history of Christianity, credited with spreading the message of Christ through his travels around the Mediterranean, and to have initially espoused the doctrine that developed as the Christian faith. Just as much as Christians see Christ through the prism of Paul's teaching, we may also see the active unfolding of Christ's message of universal brotherhood, translated today as social justice or human rights through the spectrum of Fr. Mike's engagements with the poor. Ardently devoted to Jesus, a passionate propagator of the faith, Paul's anguish and self-reflection is clearly depicted in his letters, contained in the Pauline correspondence and in Acts in the Holy Bible. These characteristics well describe Michael Paul Rodrigo, who went through similarly intense agonizing, contemplation, and inner torment across his spiritual life, culminating in profound spiritual transformations as he strove to fulfil his true calling on a journey for justice.

The dramatic conversion of Paul (previously known as Saul of Tarsus, the Jewish scholar and legalist) on the road to Damascus serves thus as an apt metaphor for the spiritual metamorphoses that his name sake, Fr. Michael Paul Rodrigo underwent across his life span, albeit with a few exceptions. While Paul the apostle's conversion came through the life changing encounter with Christ as an adult, Fr. Mike's spiritual journey started in his childhood. His immense sense of altruism and devotion to Jesus Christ would have been rooted in the extraordinary faith environment that Fr. Mike grew up in, while its blossoming can be attributable to the divine call he heard and followed faithfully across his life.

Furthermore, each apogee of his faith journey portends the immensely transformative dynamics of his life trajectory: his veneration of Mary, Mother of God in the aftermath of his mother's passing early in his life; the decision in his late teens to enter the priesthood; the insidious poverty he agonizingly witnessed as a theological teacher in his early thirties; the impassioned soul searching that led him to question the unjust structuring of society; and finally, his physical transition to the remote rural area of Buttala in his early fifties to engage directly with the poor and present the liberative role and message of Jesus Christ to the Buddhist poor. Like Paul, and similar to Jesus himself, Fr. Mike sought "unbelievers," and was pressured and persecuted by hostile forces along his life journey. Through it all, he demonstrated selfless courage, self-renunciation, a deep compassion for the suffering and injustices endured by the poor, experienced the anguish of abandonment as plots grew against him, and yet persisted in what he perceived as a sacred duty—accepting suffering and risking death as the ultimate sacrifice in his quest for social justice.

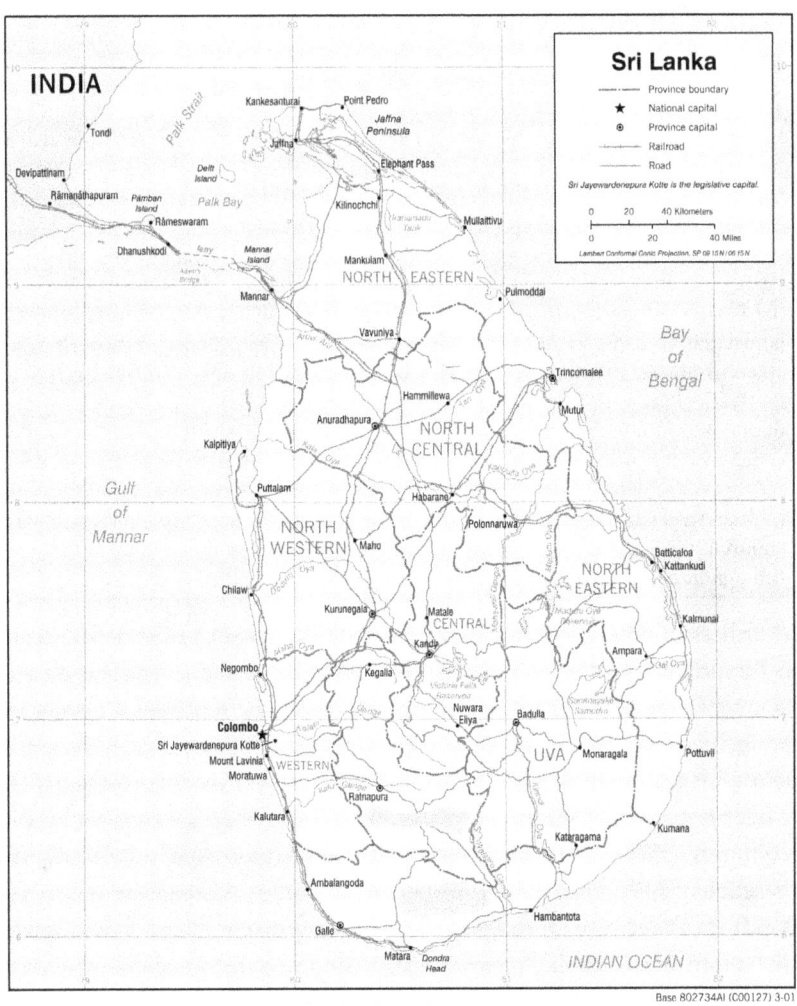

AMBASSADOR FOR CHRIST: EMBRACING DIVERSITY

Hailing originally from the southern town of Galle, like many in that era, the Rodrigo family was of mixed faith. Richard, Fr. Mike's father, came from a Methodist family and converted to Catholicism when he married Georgiana. Similar to most mixed-faith families in Sri Lanka, all available accounts indicate that in the Rodrigo family there was a seamless accommodation of diverse faith beliefs practiced by family members, possibly attributable to the cultural tendency to accept and embrace loved ones,

> **Roots of Faith:**
> **Historical Significance of Galle**
>
> The southern coastal city of Galle was the largest city in Sri Lanka across four centuries of colonial rule, and the earliest European administrative center. It was also a major port city until the British shifted the port to Colombo. Believed to be Tarshish of the Old Testament, Galle was the conduit of a thriving trade in rare luxuries, including precious metals and stones, ivory, elephants, and spices (i.e., cinnamon, cardamom, etc.). It was used by ancient mariners, from Arab merchant vessels to Portuguese explorers plying the ancient sea-lanes of the so-called "Orient." In 1505, the Portuguese, the main European maritime power of the day, colonized the island and introduced Catholicism. The country came under Dutch control during the 1600s as the result of the Indo-Dutch wars and the Dutch Reform Church gained a foothold, along with the introduction of Protestantism. Galle thus became the site of the oldest Protestant church in Sri Lanka, the *Groote Kerk*. Even after power was ceded to the British in 1796, Galle continued as the chief port for goods and passengers alike. Despite the diverse faith influences, and across four hundred years of colonial rule, which included mass (often coerced) conversions, Buddhist traditions endured in Galle. Residents of Galle simply accommodated the multiple influences through interfaith marriages that seemed to overlook the differences.

regardless of differences in faith and creed. The source of his early interest in Buddhism and the reason why he pursued a deeper understanding of its tenets later in life can thus be traced to close encounters with extended family members of diverse faiths. As he clarified to the author a few months before his untimely demise in 1987, the mere fact that there was such an easy, if not amiable intermingling of individuals who adhered to the two seemingly different faith traditions of Sri Lanka impressed him deeply. The presence of his paternal aunt in the family home, as an active, practicing Buddhist, is a testament to this high level of accommodation. Although he was raised as a Catholic, young Michael accompanied his paternal aunt to the local Buddhist temple, where he had the opportunity to observe Buddhist practices and learn about the Buddhist belief system. At home, certain aspects of Buddhism that he witnessed first-hand had made an impression on him. Observing as a young boy, the serene countenance of his aunt immersed in her daily meditation practice in an utterly peaceful demeanor had peaked in him a curiosity about Buddhist tenets early on. No doubt the contentious history of Christianity in Sri Lanka,[4] including the efforts of

---

4. See Pinto, "Sri Lanka, a Brief History of Christianity," for a discussion on the destruction of Buddhist temples and forced conversions by Portuguese Catholic colonizers in the 1500s; the Dutch colonizers' persecution of Catholics in the 1600s (after they assumed rule of Sri Lanka, then referred to as Seylan) and their efforts to ban Catholicism (in an effort to impose Protestantism); the eviction of local priests who had converted to

missionary activities to suppress Buddhism made the particular experience of interfaith harmony among his own extended family a source of much inspiration for Fr. Mike, as confirmed by his niece.

> I think Michael *baappa*[5] witnessed first-hand how Buddhists and Christians can live in harmony and this would have made a great impression on a young boy.[6]

The careful adherence to the Buddhist principle of *ahimsa* (nonviolence) extended to all sentient beings is yet another enduring impression that would have shaped young Michael's perspectives on Buddhism. The *ahimsa* practiced in the Rodrigo home even in risky situations is captured in the following anecdote recounted by Ms. Solomons:

> One Poya[7] day when my grand aunt was meditating, a centipede had crawled into the room. When family members tried to kill it, she forbade them and tried valiantly to shoo it out. Unfortunately, during this process, the centipede had grabbed her finger and dug in its claws deep to the point that she was in severe pain. She was nonetheless undeterred in her continued adherence to ahimsa.[8]

Many who knew him at a young age recall that the beliefs and rituals of Buddhism, also observed during his visits to his paternal ancestral home in Galle, were a source of fascination for him. The influence of these cultural roots in accommodating multiple faiths is acknowledged by Fr. Mike. His dear friend and collaborator, the late Rev. Fr. Tissa Balasuriya, also a tireless advocate and promoter of social justice, recalls Fr. Mike saying,

---

Catholicism, including through brutal means such as flogging; and the stance of superiority assumed by British colonial officers (after the country was ceded to British power in 1815) who not only looked down upon Buddhism and local faith practices, but also condemned them as inferior rituals adhered to by "heathens." Historical records also cite other actions that reflected discriminatory tactics toward the Buddhist masses. These include the violation of the treaty of 1815 in which the British had promised to safeguard Buddhism, including a declaration of its rites and ceremonies as sacred and inviolate, the prohibitions imposed upon the Buddhist population denying them privileges accessible to the small Christian population, and the public disparagement of Buddhism as a vulgar following of ignorant natives.

5. Sinhala term for father's younger brother (uncle).
6. Devayani Solomons, personal communication to the author, April 2016.
7. Full moon days considered sacred by the Buddhists in Sri Lanka.
8. Devayani Solomons, personal communication to the author, April 2016.

> My father hailed from a Buddhist/Methodist milieu in the south of Sri Lanka and my closest relations are from Buddhism and Methodism, and so wishing to be an ecumenist, I started Buddhist-Christian dialogue very early.[9]

Yet another influential figure in Fr. Mike's early life, who would have inculcated early knowledge of Buddhism and no doubt imbued in him an affinity with the Buddhist faith is a young man from the southern town of Matara, Mr. Pieris Aaron Nagasinghe (born 1895) who resided in the Rodrigo home from 1928 (a year after Fr. Mike was born) for a dozen years. Fr. Mike would have on occasion accompanied him to the Buddhist temple as a young boy—something he apparently relished.[10] Referred to as "elder brother" (*Aiya*) in the Rodrigo household, Mr. Nagasinghe was clearly a well-loved and influential figure across Fr. Mike's life. As family members recall, Fr. Mike consulted him at each major step in his religious career, including his initial decision to join the priesthood, his plans to travel to Rome for his first doctorate, and his decision in 1980 to serve the Buddhist poor in Buttala. In turn, as his daughter Mrs. Nanda Wijesekere recalls, Mr. Nagasinghe had provided constant encouragement and moral support at each step of Fr. Mike's faith journey.

> For those whom He foreknew, He also predestined to become conformed to the image of His Son, so that He would be the firstborn among many brethren; and these whom He predestined, He also called; and these whom He called, He also justified; and these whom He justified, He also glorified.
>
> —Rom 8:29.

FAITH FORMATION: THE SEED SANCTIFIED

From a young age, not only did Fr. Mike thrive in a spiritually nurturing environment, but his faith journey shows evidence of early spiritual growth, symbolic of the sanctification[11] needed to enter fully into a religious life. As in the parable of the sower (Matt 13:3–9) which illustrates the vital role of a nurturing environment in the growth of a seed, in Fr. Mike's life we see

---

9. Rodrigo, quoted in Balasuriya, "Fr. Michael Rodrigo OMI., Prophet & Martyr," 4.

10. Recounted by Nanda Nagasinghe (now Mrs. Wijesekere), based on her recollections of stories told by her father.

11. The formation of God's image in us.

evidence of the conduciveness of his familial milieu in preparing him to embark on his journey of faith. Rittenbaugh argues that

> with sanctification, Christ's righteousness actually, literally becomes ours through the process of obedience, overcoming, prayer, study, producing fruit, sacrificing ourselves, serving, being led and enabled by God's Holy Spirit, as He purifies our heart and infuses within us His divine nature—thus producing His image and *holiness*.[12]

Christian theology recognizes two key elements in faith formation: inherited faith through family faith traditions, and the "imitation" of faith through internalization and integration of faith beliefs, concepts, and practices. Faith is thus understood as something that deepens and grows over time.

Although it may seem that a biography is an ill-fitting form to delve into a discussion of the theories of faith development, I pause here to highlight the currents of thought on this topic in order to illustrate the significance of the early influences in Fr. Mike's faith journey. The variant strands of theorizing on faith development put forward models that endeavor to map individual progression in faith across life. These models can be categorized into several types: life span theories, structural stage theories, or dialectical/socio-psychological theories.

The process by which early faith formation occurs has been the subject of much study by psychologists, religious studies scholars and theologians alike. The classic text in this regard is by psychologist James Fowler,[13] who put forward a theory of faith development proceeding in linear progression through six stages life: "Primal Faith," during the period of infancy and early childhood; "Intuitive-Projective Faith," common among young children; "Mythic-Literal Faith," ascribable to the pre-adolescent years; "Synthetic-Conventional Faith," during adolescence; "Individuative-Reflective Faith," in post-adolescence; "Conjunctive Faith," around mid-life; and "Universalizing Faith," culminating in a transcendent stage of transformative belief. Although Fowler's work is recognized by theologians, religious educators, and professionals, it is utilized primarily in theological empiricism or pastoral care. It has also been the subject of controversy mainly due to concerns about its empirical applicability, as well as cultural relevance. With regard to Fr. Mike's faith formation, it appears that his faith journey would have adhered quite closely to each of Fowler's stages.

---

12. Rittenbaugh, "Balanced Doctrine and Application," para. 43.
13. Fowler, *Faith Development and Pastoral Care*.

CALL TO FAITH

> "The priesthood is not a vocation, it is a calling."
>
> —Thomas Benjamin Cooray, OMI (First Cardinal of Sri Lanka), undated.

The divine call to faith as the primary impetus to embarking on a spiritual vocation is a key theological concern. Often referred to as the "summons" to serve, taking on the priestly vocation is considered a response to a divine call, registered in the Latin *vocare,* to call, from which this verb is derived. As the Apostle John proclaims the call from God, "You have not chosen Me, but I have chosen you" (John 15:16). Unlike other vocations, embracing the vocation of priesthood entails the acceptance and response to Christ's call to follow him, and to guide others to Jesus. It is through this insight that we may understand Fr. Mike's calling as a priest early on. The sparse availability of information on his early spirituality makes it a challenging task to trace the primary influences in Fr. Mike's faith formation. Despite the absence of a personal account, drawing from available anecdotal evidence, the following discussion puts forward some plausible factors that would have provided the impetus to his early spiritual stirrings.

Few details are available on the call to faith that Fr. Mike would have experienced early on. Nonetheless, a review of his faith trajectory makes it obvious that he was called by the divine at a young age, and that he followed unhesitatingly. It is also clear that he did so passionately, with unfailing devotion and commitment. Despite the absence of a first-hand narrative attesting to such a divine call in his early years, the fact that he chose to work closely with faith community associations since the age of fourteen clearly evinces his heeding to such a call. As evident from his theological insights (discussed in chapter 3) and the various practical endeavors he embarked on to advance social justice across the course of his life, we may deduce that he certainly felt called for a divine purpose, just as much the Apostle Paul confirms his calling, "Paul, *called* as an apostle of Jesus Christ by the will of God"(1 Cor 1).

Early Life

Friends of the Rodrigo family who knew Fr. Mike as a young boy recall that even as a young child, he was very religious. Throughout his school years, he had demonstrated an interest in the priesthood. He served as an altar boy at St. Mary's Church, Dehiwela, during his primary school years at the Parish School of Dehiwela, was part of the choir, and became a youth faith leader in Boys Town Dehiwela (in his designated role as a "mayor"). Young Michael's secondary education was undertaken at St. Peter's College, Dehiwela. He was already immersed in youth faith formation at both institutions, where he organized sports activities, drama, and faith discussions. A comment by his colleague, the late Fr. Tissa Balasuriya, reveals Fr. Mike's early leanings toward selflessness. "At Dehiwela as a boy he was Mayor of Boys Town. At a youthful age, he already showed dedication and leadership. He used to encourage youth to give themselves to concern for others."[14]

Echoing these thoughts, one of the boys who participated in Boys Town, Dehiwela, had this to say:

> To me, he was the person who taught the rudiments of poster drawing. That to a person who had very little understanding of art. And the posters were to expose to the community the injustices in society. His crusade for social justice. His many lessons I remember with gratitude and fondness.[15]

Certainly an influential faith leader in Fr. Mike's early life was Fr. Romauld Fernando, the parish priest at St. Mary's Church, Dehiwela, his home parish. According to family members, Fr. Romauld recognized and nurtured

14. Balasuriya, "He Paid the Supreme Price," 12.
15. Ibid., 14.

> **Boys Town Dehiwela**
>
> Modeled after the old Christian association for boys established in the United States, Boys Town (BT) was set up in 1938 by Fr. Romauld Fernando, OMI, in the Parish of St. Mary's Dehiwela, Sri Lanka. Although the original intention of BT, as it was envisaged in the US was to guide and direct youth from underprivileged homes toward a moral life and to avert their path to juvenile delinquency, the BT chapter in Dehiwela catered to the education of parish boys, mostly middle-class, on conducting themselves in a Christian manner. It also supported, however, boys of lesser means in the area.
>
> Fr. Romauld was the "governor," and local youth were elected as "mayors," assigned responsibility for various activities: altar service, the youth choir, sports meets, competitive games such as cricket matches, and other such activities. Fr. Romauld instilled in the young members a motto, still remembered by many: "This is my church. . . . It gives me life, forms me, and is the constant reminder that Jesus is with me. Looking after it is my responsibility."

the exceptional personal qualities in young Michael Rodrigo. St. Mary's Church, Dehiwela, is still one of the largest parishes in Sri Lanka, both in structure and membership. St. Mary's was also the seat of a Eucharistic Rally in 1945, the first ever to be held in the pre-independence country. Fr. Mike would have been eighteen years old at that point, and this landmark event would have been one that sealed young Mike's intention to join the priesthood. Prior to that, another critical event had already stamped a conviction in his heart about his life direction.

> Fr. Mike belongs to a generation that was born in the days of colonial rulers, was educated in the English medium at St. Peter's College and lived through the 1950s where there was much critique of the Church for "Catholic Action" and the crisis of the Schools Take Over in 1960–61. He reflected on all these and saw the need of being closer to the people as a priest and religions. His interest in "Social Justice" was aroused by the movement and paper begun by Fr. Peter Pillai when he was at St. Peter's College. In the 1960s and 1970s the Church and the Oblate Congregation took clear options in favour of the poor, of Social Justice, of Peace and dialogue with the other Religions.
>
> —Balasuriya, "Fr. Michael Rodrigo OMI," 4.

MATURING IN FAITH

The turning point in Fr. Mike's spiritual journey, in terms of a full commitment to a religious life, came with the passing away of his mother at a young age. His cousin (and only surviving relative of his generation), Merrill J. Fernando remembers how young Michael was shattered upon the death of his mother, as he was very close to her. Fr. Mike's own personal notes (undated) include a mention of the sadness that engulfed him upon his mother's death. Lost in his sorrow, he recalls how he sat on the beach watching the waves crashing against the shore for days on end, coming away with the conclusion that life is just as fragile as the waves that dispersed on the beach. Thus, the decision to devote his life to the Lord had emerged. A deeper clarification on this matter in Fr. Mike's notes offers a glimpse of the first stirrings of his heart to follow a religious life, and what prompted him to choose the Oblates of Mary Immaculate (OMI) order:

> My mother died when I was young. I did not know what to do. I was just going around. I felt lost without my mother. At this time, a priest introduced me to the devotion of our Lady. From that time on, Our Lady has become my mother and this is one reason why I became an Oblate.[16]

Upon completing his secondary studies, Michael served as a member of the teaching staff at St. Peter's College for a short spell. It was soon after that, at the age of twenty, he made a decision to enter the priesthood, entering the Oblate Novitiate[17] on September 1, 1947, in the town of Bambalapitiya, a few kilometers from his hometown Dehiwela. Six years hence, in 1954, he was ordained as part of the OMI congregation. Recognized as one of the brightest seminarians, he was chosen, together with his close friend, the late Fr. Dalston Forbes, OMI, to study at the Gregorian University in Rome. Little information is available on his years in Rome, except for impressions recorded through his poems, available in a published collection (Harris, 1988).

> **Missionary Oblates of Mary Immaculate (OMI)**
>
> The OMI is a Roman Catholic congregation founded by St. Eugene de Mazenod in approximately 1816, formally approved by Pope Leo XII in 1826. Dedicated to working among the poor, the OMI motto is, "He has sent me to evangelize the poor." This central commitment to serving the poor would have been a key factor in its appeal to Fr. Michael Rodrigo, in addition to the devotion to Mary, mother of God that he had committed to as a young boy. The OMI congregation has been in Sri Lanka since 1847, when Oblate pioneers arrived at the port of Galle.

Upon his return to Sri Lanka in 1955, he took on a position at the National Seminary of Our Lady of Lanka, in Ampitiya (a small town adjoining the hill city of Kandy) as lecturer in theological studies until 1971. During this time, he completed his PhD thesis,[18] earning his first doctorate in Buddhist

---

16. Refers to a member of the Roman Catholic Order of priests, the Oblates of Mary Immaculate (OMI). Rodrigo, no date, referenced in Forbes, "Martyr for Social Justice."

17. The institution where novices of the Order of Oblates of Mary Immaculate (OMI) resided for their clerical training.

18. See Rodrigo, "Some Aspects of the Enlightenment."

philosophy in 1959. The choice of this topic was influenced a great deal by the decrees of Vatican II, which called for an indigenization and contextualization of faith. At that time, in the early 1960s, Fr. Mike became part of a handful of Christian theologians to put forward some seemingly radical notions about grounding faith practice in the cultural realities of the masses. Subsequently, in 1971, he felt compelled to deepen his reflections and analysis of the parallel conceptualizations of selflessness in Buddhism and Christianity. He decided to enroll in a course of study at the Institut Catholique in Paris, France,[19] where he further developed his ideas on the concept of Passover, incorporated into his second doctoral thesis.[20] Chapter 2 continues the next steps in the extraordinary journey of faith that Fr. Mike followed.

PERSONAL PROFILE: CRUSADER FOR JUSTICE, PRIEST, POET, PASSIONATE ADVOCATE FOR THE POOR

Many adjectives are used to describe Fr. Mike, providing a glimpse of the enduring personal traits that characterized him as priest, scholar, theologian, and ardent activist for social justice. The personal attributes most remembered include his characteristic joviality, his warm and caring nature, his deep compassion for the poor and downtrodden, and passion for right action, in addition to his charismatic personality. All who knew him at the time recall his quick wit and jovial personality that endeared him to many. One individual who had been a member at Boys Town, Dehiwela, under Fr. Mike's tutelage recalls, "Some of the most endearing qualities were his mischievous smile and jovial banter. Sharp and quick witted, he would make any stranger feel at ease."[21] This is echoed in the words of the late Fr. Derrick Mendis, SJ, a dear friend of Fr. Mike who traveled to Buttala often while Fr. Mike was alive and was one of the first priests upon the scene soon after his murder.

> Endowed with a sparkling sense of humour, he added lustre to his conversations and talks, with gems of wit. To me, this was one of the most endearing qualities of this great man.[22]

---

19. Fr. Mike thankfully acknowledges the role of the Oblate provincial director of the time, Father Lucien Schmitt, OMI, "who made it possible for me to go to Paris' Catholic Institute for this dissertation from 1971–1973" in his dissertation. See Rodrigo, "Moral Passover," vii.

20. See Rodrigo, "Moral Passover."

21. Perera, "For a Younger Disciple," 14.

22. Editorial in the *Island* newspaper, Colombo, Sri Lanka, November 27, 1987.

CARITAS PERSONIFIED: FAMILY TIES

It could be easily argued that Fr. Mike personified the concept of "caritas" in the sense of unconditional, self-sacrificing love, captured in the popular hymn "Ubi Caritas est vera, Deus ibi est."[23] Glimpses of this are offered through the letters that he wrote over the years to his siblings and nieces, as well as from their personal recollections. What emerges from these exchanges is an enduring profile of Fr. Mike as a sensitive, caring, tender-hearted person, with tremendous love for his family, his nation, and the downtrodden of the world. These letters reveal his thoughtfulness in speaking to their life concerns, the guidance and wisdom he offered, a dash of humor and a witty repartee thrown in to the mixture, typically signed, "Yours lovingly, Michael."

In one letter to his sister Petronella, dated June 30, 1968, on the occasion of his forty-first birthday, he acknowledges the special bond between the two

> No wonder I told you some days ago that you'll always be my best Akka.[24] I love the others very much, but not more than you. For you there's a special little place. . . . I can never repay you, and it is for that, that I try to love the little ones who are an extension of you &[25] Arthur. I ask for long life for you, Aiya,[26] Loku Akka, & Beata & all yours.[27]

The stream of letters to Petronella suggest that after his mother passed away, she took on a motherly role with him as we learn from yet another letter to her dated January 11, 1967, where he recalls one such memory from his childhood: "You hugged me on the shoulder or your hip, and showed me the beautiful trees and flowers in God's creation. I remember it as yesterday."[28]

As a revered figure in the extended family circle, he maintained ties not only to his immediate family, but also to distant cousins and their children. Hiranthi De Silva, one of Fr. Mike's cousins' daughters recalls that he made regular visits to look in on them, to ensure that they were

---

23. Referencing the words of the Apostle Paul to the Corinthians (first letter), these words (loosely translated as "where there is love, God is there") are the equivalent of love (as in fraternal/human love) to the presence of God.

24. Honorific in Sinhala to indicate elder sister.

25. Fr. Mike had a habit of using the ampersand to denote the word "and," indicative of how pressed for time he was, but the effort he made nonetheless to communicate regularly with his family members.

26. Honorific in Sinhala to indicate elder brother.

27. Rodrigo, letter to Petronella, June 30, 1968.

28. Rodrigo, letter to Petronella, January 11, 1967.

educated at the best schools, and that they were getting the health care they needed. He remembered each of their birthdays and addressed them in endearing terms, often using the adjective *sudu*, an expression of affection common in the culture. When Petronella's eldest child was born, Fr. Mike, then studying in Italy proposed the name "Eulalie," an anglocization of the Italian name Eulalia, for a girl born close to Christmas (Yuletide). He had devised unique descriptors for each of his nieces and nephews, assigned to fit a special trait or attribute he would have observed in each. Shantini (his elder brother Sam's daughter) is referred to as "noble hearted," Eulalie is heralded for her courage and steadfastness, and her younger sister Marie, fondly referred to as "Marie Biscuits," alluding to her manner of providing short and crisp answers, reminiscent of a well-loved brand of biscuits[29] in Sri Lanka. Michael (Sam's elder son) who bears his name is characterized as magnanimous, with a golden heart. Love of and fascination with nature is observed of Richard, the younger of Sam's sons. These characterizations of each family member reveals his observant, tender appreciation of each. In a letter dated October 13, 1986 to his brother Sam, wishing him and his wife on the occasion of their thirty-fifth wedding anniversary, Fr. Mike writes,

> For my dear, dear Aiya and my dear, dear Dorothy Akka, on your Happy Wedding Anniversary Day of 1986, and for the lovely brood of friendly children God raised for this world through you. A special Shantini whose patience matches her love, a magnanimous Michael whose name I'm proud to bear, whose golden heart turned out to be a heart of flesh. A Richie amazed at the simplest things in life and captured, enthralled not by loads of money but by a lovely tree, a Devi, true to her name, giving maximal delight to Maxie and the baby, a Priya, dear to the gods, happy with Lakkie and lucky with happiness.[30]

In many a letter to his family members, he bemoans the lack of enough time to spend with them.

> I am sorry in a way that when I come to your place or to the other two places it has to be not more than a flying visit. When the children were growing up, I was absent from the country;[31] when in their teens I was away on Ministry in Kandy; when in the growing

---

29. Sri Lankan term for what would be called cookies in the United States.
30. Rodrigo, letter to Sam, October 13, 1986.
31. Referring to his liturgical studies overseas in Rome and Paris.

Early Life

years, I went further in to the People's area in B'wela,[32] and when I'm distant and absent the fledglings are absent from their nests.[33]

Further on in the same letter, dated October 18, 1984 he attributes this to the demands of his priestly role. "Perhaps this is part of the price we have to pay: Part of the cost of discipleship (as Bonhoeffers says): to leave father & mother & brother & sister & house & lands, etc."[34]

Nonetheless, it is clear that he strove diligently to remain a part of his family circle in some way. He made time out of his busy schedule to accompany a niece or nephew to the doctor, to counsel a sibling, and even to offer French lessons. His letters regularly urge social action, faithful prayer and devotion, and caution against spiritual complacency. A short poem by an unknown author quoted at the end of one letter dated October 16, 1983 includes the quip: "Do noble deeds not dream them all day long . . . and let your life become one *grand sweet song*."[35]

> And Michael's prophecy was shot through and through with the brilliance and tenderness of poesy. Poesy is the art of creating a poem which is the delicate record in beautifully strung phrases of the reality beyond the appearance. Poesy needs creativity, sensitivity, vision. Michael had all these qualities.
>
> —Caspersz, "Priesthood," 18.

In another letter dated December 3, 1983 to his niece Shantini from India (where he was attending a theological meeting), he notes,

> There are so many beautiful things and "ugly" things in the world. Try to remove the "ugly" things like hatred, dissension, partisan spirit, exclusivism, over protection, and foster the kindly things like peace, patience, joy, relationships, forgiveness, rejection-of-rancour and the like.[36]

In closing, he reflects an eerie premonition on the fleeting nature of life.

> We are not going to be here on earth forever: the teardrop of the Taj, the flowing Ganges are reminiscent of the evanescence of life. How fast the days are fleeting. The end may be upon us when we least expect it & yet so many who just go on as they are. You must

---

32. Shorthand used by Fr. Mike for the town of Bandarawela, where he was a lecturer at the Sevaka Sevana Seminary.

33. Rodrigo, letter of October 18, 1984.

34. Ibid.

35. Rodrigo, letter of October 16, 1983.

36. Rodrigo, letter of December 3, 1983.

pray with all your life, not only with mind & heart. Time is short; eternity unending.[37]

Finally, a mere forty-three days before his untimely demise, a letter penned on September 28, 1987 to his eldest sister Hilda captures a poignant and prophetic commentary that perhaps portended his passing.

The cross is not something we hang on the wall or round our neck. Jesus hung on it first. It was the Roman Empire's chief instrument of political torture. So, we must be ready to die for our people if and when the time comes. He died at 33, because he stuck out his neck for people, for the poor, the down & out & distressed. Everything is political but "politics" isn't everything. So, I cannot do politics (party politics). I have to preach the Gospel—the poor are victims of injustice. They will judge you & me on the last day, for they are Jesus: "I was hungry & you gave me to eat. I was thirsty & you gave me to drink," etc.... Jesus is the poor; the poor is Jesus. That's what I think & I'm not wrong. The rich can never get to heaven unless they share: "Woe to you, rich..." Jesus said, four times. I can't help it if I am with the poor. I cannot destroy the Infant Jesus of Prague statue & also keep it. He was born as an infant to save all infants, all men & women of all time, of all places—therefore also the poor Buddhist landless, voiceless children, men & women who have no 2-story dwellings; no food, no beds, nor rooms in their homes & so very often kuruminiyas (*insects*) get into their ears.... Life is fleeting, I died long ago, the day I made my vows in 1948—it is 40 years now.[38]

POET

Gifted with a talent for writing eloquently and evocatively, Fr. Mike had developed a penchant for poetry in his early twenties. It was a testament to his sensitivity to the world around him, and his finely tuned perceptive capacities. By the age of twenty-five, he had composed forty seven poems, compiled in 1952 under a collection entitled *Stardust in the Waves*. As the editor of a collection of his poetry, Elizabeth Harris[39] notes,

---

37. Ibid.
38. Rodrigo, letter of September 28, 1987.
39. Dr. Harris is a specialist in Religious Studies, and holds a specialism in Buddhist Studies, and Inter-Faith Studies.

Early Life

The poems show a sensitive person steeped in traditional Christian theology. An intense yearning to understand the suffering of Christ is present. The symbols of darkness and light, flame and water are used. Christ's sacrifice is a burning, flaming circle of light. Inner turmoil is the darkness of a cave when light is withdrawn.[40]

Over the next two decades, as he advanced along his spiritual journey, his poetry evolved to capture his encounters with the rural poor and his observations of their suffering. The poems he composed of these encounters speak to how he witnessed Christ among the poor—Christ's persecution, his suffering, and his surrender. In this way, he saw the "human face of God"[41] among the poor, and vice versa, the representation of Christ in the poor. He was able to connect the seemingly mundane daily rhythms of village life to a deeper understanding of the eternal cycles of life. Many of the poems capture the despair, injustice and anguish of those trapped in poverty. Most reflect a symbolic inflection, infused with his interpretations of the significance of the travail and distress endured by them. He seems to have extracted a fundamental truth from each incident, and woven his quest for justice into each poem. The tenderness alluded to his poetry by Fr. Mike's good friend Fr. Paul Caspersz (see quotation above) is evident in each of them. A lovely little poem written quickly in the wee hours of the morning for his grandniece Hilani (left) offers a glimpse of the depths of his tenderness and the manner in which his words were intertwined with the deeper spiritual aspirations he held for those he loved.

> *Whose little sandals, these, Lord*
> *Whose little sandals, please?*
> *I guess they are Hilani's*
> *Whose little feet are shod.*
>
> *And when she wears them, please Lord*
> *Bring home the truth to her*
> *That many are unshod, Lord*
> *Their bare feet walk forever*
>
> *Through barren, empty waste land*
> *Or owned by foreign heart*
> *That cruel have, in one band,*
> *Made peasants rightful smart.*
>
> *The cows that gave the leather, Lord*
> *Have their milk all lured away*
> *The few unthinking hearts, Lord*
> *Think the world is theirs today.*
>
> *And now may this girl, humble*
> *Wend fearless mighty way, Lord*
> *To redress wrongs and lighten load*
> *Of many, many astray.*
>
> *With walking feet and seeing eyes*
> *And gentle step, the way*
> *May he and she help all rise*
> *Unto that glorious day.*
>
> —Rodrigo, in Harris, "Tissues," 69.

---

40. Harris, "Double Belonging," 82.
41. Rodrigo, "Pieta," line 37, in Harris, "Tissues," 46.

2

Engagements in Faith
Liturgical Leader, Teacher, and Social Justice Activist

> By his life, work, and example, Mike has outlined for us a model to be emulated by every priest who wishes to be an effective instrument of Christ.
>
> —Mendis, "Appreciation," 42.

AT THE MERE AGE of twenty-one, Michael Paul Rodrigo made his first profession of vows, on September 8, 1948. That same year, he and his close friend and fellow priest, the late Fr. Dalston Forbes was selected to pursue higher studies at the International Scholasticate in Rome, Italy, where he undertook his ecclesiastical studies.[1] This selection was based on the intellectual gifts and scholarly potential of the candidates, in keeping with Oblate practice. Even at that young age, Br. Mike was clearly showing his strong intellectual bent and incisive analysis of liturgical texts. He was ordained a priest on July 4, 1954 in Rome and subsequently completed his post-graduate studies in 1959, focusing his PhD on Buddhist principles through the lens of the teachings of St. Thomas Aquinas.[2]

---

1. Details acquired from copy of a speech made by Mr. Cecil Jayawardana, on the occasion of the Silver Jubilee of the ordination of Frs. Michael Rodrigo and Dalston Forbes, published in the St. Mary's Church, Dehiwela.

2. See Rodrigo, "Some Aspects of the Enlightenment."

Engagements in Faith

THE AMPITIYA YEARS: SCHOLAR AND TEACHER

> Fr. Michael Rodrigo served on the teaching staff under Fr. Fred Sacket, OMI, the First Rector of the National Seminary of Our Lady of Lanka at Ampitiya, newly inaugurated in 1955. Fr. Sacket was a Texan specialist in Education, who initiated the training and formation of the first batches of students for the Catholic priesthood and gave a solid leadership to the teaching staff and left his imprint on the formation of the future Catholic priests of Sri Lanka.
>
> —Ceylon Today, "Fr. Michael Rodrigo OMI," para. 1.

In September 1955, Fr. Mike returned to Sri Lanka and was immediately assigned to the teaching staff of the newly formed National Seminary in Ampitiya, which was under the charge of the Oblates. The rector at the time, Fr. Fred Sackett, OMI, originating from Texas, tasked him with teaching liturgy, comparative religion, Buddhism, and psychology to hundreds of seminarians. Throughout his twenty-two-year residence at Ampitiya, Fr. Mike expanded his teaching repertoire to include philosophy, cosmology, logic, and interreligious dialogue. He soon established himself as a well-loved and admired teacher and spiritual mentor. He is known to have exerted a powerful influence on the seminarians because of his extraordinary sincerity and devotion, his passion for Christ, and his compassion for the poor.

Across the seminary, his appeal as a teacher was notably due to his deeply spiritual nature, his exceptional intellect, and his broad knowledge base, considered inspirational on all counts. "He was highly educated and deeply prayerful, which sharpened our intellect and inspired us to emulate him."[3] It was his unique manner of imparting the knowledge that the seminarians unvaryingly appreciated, his lectures punctuated with his customary humor and jovial comportment. Some who went on to become leading clerical figures, such as Fr. Winston Fernando, OMI (PhD), Bishop of Badulla, have recollections in this regard.

> In the Roman Catholic Church he was regarded as the leader of liturgical renewal of the sixties.
>
> —Fernando, "True Practitioner," 18.

> He was quick-witted and his sense of humor made his classes interesting. Being a teacher of liturgy and a liturgist at the National Seminary, Ampitiya, Fr. Mike spearheaded the liturgical renewal in Sri Lanka following the Second Vatican Council. He had a permanent liturgical exhibition at the Seminary and published a "Liturgical Lifeline" Bulletin for the benefit of the Clergy and Religious in the island.[4]

> He was often seen, clad in pure snow white dress, walking briskly the short distance between the Oblate Scholasticate and the National Seminary, Ampitiya, hugging a stack of books and notes for the classes where he so loved to impart the knowledge he acquired in Rome, Paris, and in daily life to the students and people. Though very busy and involved in numerous new projects, he never missed an occasion to listen to a worker in the seminary gardens, help solve an interacting problem in the community and take time to discuss life situations with scholastics and seminarians in a very positive manner.
>
> —Dharmasena, "Appreciation," para. 1.

---

3. Archbishop Cardinal Malcolm Ranjith, personal account, personal interview, July 26, 2016.

4. Fernando, "Message," 11.

Engagements in Faith

Another reason for his popularity would have been due to the innovative pedagogical strategies he devised, which were more interactive learning than by rote, well ahead of his time. As another of his former students attests,

> In the methodology and liturgy classes he taught, he was a conscientious teacher and a disciplinarian. Should he observe a little sign of impertinence in the class, he would quip, smilingly of course, "Beware, there are two ways to be popular, but alas, one is very cheap!" Long before the computers appeared, he taught his students the methods to "computerize" diverse information on square cards classified in alphabetical order. His liturgical innovations thrilled many in the two seminaries.[5]

He thus came to be heralded as one of the leading educationists among the Catholic clergy in the country, and was invited to participate in discussions and conferences across the Asia region. Most of all, it was his charisma and accessibility that seems to have left an indelible impression on many, as Fr. Winston Fernando, OMI, recalls:

> He was also available to students who wished to consult him on various matters connected to their academic studies or to personal

5. Dharmasena, "Appreciation," para. 2

or spiritual matters about which students went to him for guidance and advice. His interest in the seminary students was not confined to academic aspects only. He joined us on hikes and for mountain climbing and these were occasions we looked forward to as students because they were so enjoyable while the many and varied informal and friendly discussions we had on the way also opened our minds to the multi-faceted splendorous world we live in.[6]

> He could not stay where he was. God got a hold of him and led him into a new adventure of the spirit. He was obedient to the heavenly vision and he went forth in faith and trust, not knowing where he was going, only knowing the One who was guiding him, into whose hands he had committed his life and his future. God led him into a new kind of ministry. His perceptions and priorities began to change.
>
> —Perera, "Message at the Funeral Service," 12.

During this time, the Vatican II discussions in Rome were gathering momentum. As the Catholic Church prepared for a broader role in shepherding humanity, the shift to ecumenism emerged, later outlined in the Decree on the Mission Activity of the Church (December 7, 1965): "Let them be educated in the ecumenical spirit, and duly prepared for fraternal dialogue with non-Christians."[7] One aspect of this call that resonated with Fr. Mike's personal faith journey was the anchoring of liturgical training in the local culture—the idea that the preparation of priests should be contextualized in the local.

> All this demands that studies for the priesthood be undertaken, so far as possible, in association and living together with their own people.[8]

Recognizing its significance for the diverse cultural and spiritual context of Sri Lanka, Fr. Mike's response appears to have been to begin formulating a conceptualization of the relevance and significance of dialogue in its many forms for the nation—its philosophical roots, the nature and significance of interfaith

> Fr. Mike was deeply involved in the liturgical apostolate as a young priest. He carried out a veritable campaign for the meaningful participation of the people in the liturgy. The reforms of Vatican II spurred him on to even further effort. But, as time went on, he matured as an Oblate priest and realized the importance of the social apostolate.
>
> —Forbes, "Martyr," 11.

---

6. Fernando, "Message," 11.
7. John XXIII, *Princeps Pastorum*, note 21.
8. Ibid., note 22.

dialogue, the "dialogue of presence," and the "dialogue of life." Letters written to family members during this time reveal his innovative approaches and his delight when his ideas were received favorably. In a letter dated July 1, 1968, addressed to his brother-in-law Arthur (Petronella's husband), he details some of the activities that he undertook at that time.

> On a rainy Saturday afternoon, I had to go to Peradeniya Training College, say Mass for them and end the day giving a lecture to a crowded hall of over three hundred teachers and visitors on "The Philosophy of Dialogue." Thank God, it was very well received even by the fifty Buddhists present in the hall, for they asked me many questions and showed real appreciation at the answers. Wasn't I even invited to take *Sil*[9] with them next time.[10]

THE SUMMONS OF VATICAN II (THE SECOND VATICAN COUNCIL)

The Second Vatican Council, commonly referred to as Vatican II, announced by Pope John XXIII in the early 1960s gathered together nearly 2,500 bishops and thousands of observers, auditors, sisters, laymen, and laywomen at St. Peter's Basilica between 1962 and 1965. The purpose of Vatican II was spiritual renewal of the church and reconsideration of the position of the church in the modern world. Organized around four sessions, Vatican II produced sixteen documents that spelled out a novel way of engaging with contemporary realities, essentially shaping a new and more "modern" direction for the Catholic Church. Each of the four sessions was devoted to one or more reform themes. Session II (September to December 1963) produced the Constitution on the Sacred Liturgy that permitted vernacularization of the liturgy. It stressed greater lay participation in the ritual and introduced a decree on the medium of social communication.

According to Georgetown University professor Fr. John W. O'Malley,[11] reconciliation was a key theme of the documents. For the first time in its history, the Catholic Church validated the principle of religious freedom and rejected all forms of civil discrimination based on religious grounds.

---

9. The word "sil" refers to the Buddhist practice of observing the precepts, usually through meditation and taking meals before the noon hour. Capitalization was in the original letter.
10. Rodrigo, letter of July 1, 1968.
11. See O'Malley, *What Happened*.

This entailed honoring the spirit of the ecumenical tradition, calling for Catholics to pray with other Christian denominations, and dialogue with other faith traditions.[12] It also included opening the Mass to symbols and traditions of non-Western cultures. An important reconciliatory move, it was credited to have played a key role in the growth of the church in Africa and parts of Asia. Respect for Judaism and Islam as Abrahamic faiths akin to Christianity was also emphasized by the Council. As Peter A. Huff (Xavier University) notes,

> Pope John wanted to reinforce that missionary mandate, but he also wanted to create an environment of dialogue, where the church would engage in all the forces of the modern world.[13]

Vatican II specifically called for the cultural contextualization of theology and the church's engagement with people of all nations. Chapter II of the Decree on the Mission Activity of the Church (December 7, 1965) makes special mention of this call:

> Therefore, let the minds of the students be kept open and attuned to an acquaintance and an appreciation of their own nation's culture. In their philosophical and theological studies, let them consider the points of contact which mediate between the traditions and religion of their homeland on the one hand and the Christian religion on the other. Likewise, priestly training should have an eye to the pastoral needs of that region; and the students should learn the history, aim, and method of the Church's missionary activity, and the special social, economic, and cultural conditions of their own people.[14]

This decree lent further credence to Fr. Mike's evolving consciousness about the dire conditions of rural Sri Lanka, the church's distance from the poor, and his yearning to bridge that gap. These events seem to have culminated in a second internal transformation Fr. Mike experienced, leading him to revise his teaching to be further culturally grounded. More significantly, they seem to have paved the way for his profound inner conversions.

As Anton Meemana, PhD, a renowned young professor of philosophy and theology at Aquinas University, Sri Lanka, explained,

---

12. Benedict XV, *Maximum Illud*, para 1. See also John XXIII, *Mater et Magistra*, note 178.

13. Quoted in Teicher, "Why is Vatican II So Important?" para. 6, line 4.

14. John XXIII, *Princeps Pastorum*, note 21.

There was a profound shift in his understanding of Christianity after Vatican II. Vatican II brought with it an "anthropological shift," the idea that the gospel message should be self-appropriated to the local cultural context. This led to a profound process of inner transformation.[15]

SECOND TRANSFORMATION: CONTEXTUALIZING SELFLESSNESS AND SACRIFICE

During the early 1960s, Fr. Mike would have experienced what could be considered a second transformation—one derived from his direct encounters with the poor as he led the Ampitiya seminarians in regular excursions to impoverished village areas and delved deeper in to the roots of their poverty. To begin with, as he reflected on and contemplated the shift in the mission of the church offered by Vatican II, he would have felt compelled to enliven the liturgy with an understanding of the life experiences of the poor in the surrounding rural area. Energized by the directives of Vatican II, Fr. Mike strove to bridge theological principles with active engagement in community life, particularly among the poor.

> "Michael saw his priesthood to be at the service not of *rite*, but of *right*."
> —Caspersz, "Priesthood," 16.

His deep reflections on the call to serve the poor embedded in the Vatican II guidelines stirred in Fr. Mike not only a dissatisfaction with the customary manner of training priests solely on the liturgy, but also a desire to engage in action to redress their situation. As one Oblate priest noted, "On weekends he went to the parishes and conducted seminars on Liturgy, thus living with the people and living what he taught."[16] In this manner, Fr. Mike contextualized the liturgy and theologized on the poor. He led young seminarians to observe and study rural life, so that the liturgical teachings could be grounded in the living realities of the people.

These excursions would have provided many insights into the challenges and trials endured by the poor. No doubt he would have been deeply moved by these encounters to the point of deeper rumination on his charge as a priest. They also prompted him to revise his approach to teaching by shifting to a more contextualized method. Reportedly,[17] the shifts he introduced were not always

15. Meemana, personal interview, July 26, 2016.
16. Singarayar, "Martyr in Living," 23.
17. Personal interviews with Fr. Claude Perera OMI, July 15, 2016, and Fr. Oswald

well received by the universal church, and within the ranks of the church hierarchy in Sri Lanka at the time. Deemed to be too radical, the progressive perspectives of Ampitiya teachers, including (and perhaps especially) Fr. Mike came under scrutiny. Subsequently, in 1972 there was a temporary closure of the seminary. As the rupture began, Fr. Mike made a decision to devote time to developing his thoughts on the notion of self-sacrifice, and its parallels in Buddhism, Christianity, and other religions. At this juncture, he decided to undertake a second PhD[18] in Theology at the Institut Catholique, Paris, which he completed in 1973.

Upon completing this second doctorate, Fr. Mike returned to Sri Lanka. At the invitation of his close friend and colleague, the late Fr. Tissa Balasuriya, OMI,[19] he began working at the Centre for Society and Religion (CSR), a place energized at the time by the dynamic discussions on Vatican II, liberation theology, and Catholic social teaching. Together, they addressed issues related to poverty and human rights, and explored alternatives to the persistent class, caste, and ethnic inequities in Sri Lanka. It was a time when the teachings of liberation theology were gaining ground across the Catholic world, including in Sri Lanka, as an alternative to the more conservative ideas of the pre-Vatican II period.

> **Centre for Society and Religion**
>
> Founded in 1971 by the outspoken social critic and activist, Fr. Tissa Balasuriya OMI, the Centre for Society and Religion (CSR) was established on the premises of Fatima Church, in Maradana, Sri Lanka. CSR spearheaded research, studies, discussions, and information dissemination on the pressing social, economic, and political problems of Sri Lanka. It brought together politicians, intellectuals, academics, and students of all persuasions to discuss the problems of the day, and fostered organized interethnic and interreligious dialogue and action as a path to justice and intercommunity harmony. CSR continues to-date to rally around social justice issues with various forums and publications.

Fr. Mike was among the handful of Christian theologians in Sri Lanka for whom the radical shifts of the Second Vatican Council struck a resonating note, based on their intimate knowledge of the deep pockets of poverty, the inequities and injustices that persisted at the margins of Sri Lankan society, often hidden, sometimes masked, and regularly overlooked by the comfortable complacency or denial that seemed to afflict the mainstream

---

Firth OMI, July 26, 2016.

18. Rodrigo, "Moral Passover."

19. Himself a critic of the injustices of the day, Fr. Tissa would have seen in Fr. Mike a close collaborator whose thinking was very much aligned with his own, as both were devoted to relying on the teachings of Christ to usher social justice.

church and the middle-classes alike. Theological luminaries of Sri Lanka such as Fr. Tissa Balasuriya, Fr. Aloysius (Aloy) Pieris, and Bishop Leo Nanayakkara were quick to grasp the significance of the new Vatican directives and to articulate responses and initiate programs, each in their unique manner. Fr. Tissa, for example, devoted his energies to spreading these ideas to audiences in Sri Lanka and across Asia as one of the pioneers of the Asian theological group. He also launched programs among the poor in Sri Lanka's urban slums. Together with Fr. Mike, he was at the forefront of a novel movement emerging in the Catholic Church in Sri Lanka at that time, whose rallying call was "from the pulpit to the *palpatha*."[20] Signifying an outreach movement from the institution of the church to the humblest dwelling, it entailed a call to assume an active role in fighting social injustice beyond the safety of church premises. Fr. Aloy, through his prolific writing on the theological perspectives relevant for Asia, advanced a culturally grounded response to the persistent injustices in Sri Lanka and across the region. Bishop Leo encouraged an outreach to the poorest and most marginalized communities in rural Sri Lanka, thereby paving the way for Fr. Mike's transition to Buttala, in the heart of poverty in this island nation.

ENGAGEMENTS IN FAITH: SEVAKA SEVANA, BANDARAWELA

Thus it was that two years later, in 1978, when he was invited by Bishop Leo Nanayakkara, OSB, to direct Sevaka Sevana, the new seminary in the diocese of Badulla,[21] Fr. Mike began to put into practice the call for a living presence among the poor. This semi-rural area offered Fr. Mike the tranquility that gave him pause for reflection. Its location in Uva, the poorest province of Sri Lanka, also availed him the opportunity to learn first-hand about the struggles of the rural poor. Reflections by Fr. Reid Shelton Fernando, chaplain of the Young Christian Workers (YCW) and Christian Workers Movement (CWM) in Sri Lanka, clarify Fr. Mike's transition from Ampitiya to Sevaka Sevana.

> I first met Fr. Mike in 1962, when I joined the National Seminar Ampitiya (Kandy). He was my professor of philosophy, but he also

20. Refers to a simple dwelling where the poor reside, the equivalent of a hut.

21. The diocese of Badulla consisted of four parishes: Badulla, Bandarawela, Lunugala, and Welimada (which had been a part of the diocese of Kandy). The Sevaka Sevana seminary was established in the Bandarawela parish. See map, above.

taught logic, psychology, and Buddhism. He was a good teacher. When he left the seminary to take a sabbatical, he developed a sense of love for people, and went on to join Msgr. Leo Nanayakkara in Sevaka Sevana ("House of Ministries"), a formation center for young priests in the region of Uva Wellassa. There he remained until the bishop's death.[22]

> **Seminary of Sevaka Sevana**
>
> The new experimental seminary in the hill town of Bandarawela, Sevaka Sevana ("haven for service") was established in the mid-1970s by the late Bishop Leo Nanayakkara, intended for training in different apostolic ministries. "This Seminary was to become a unique Third World experience and a step forward in the direction of a rupture from the Western Model training factory for priests. At the start, 'the Sevakas' spent every weekend with people in some part of Uva. Soon the period of time spent with people grew longer, extending even for weeks. The idea then was to visit every little part of Uva, not with the ambition of converting others but in order to unlearn and to conscientize themselves" (Fernando, "True Practitioner," 22).
>
> Soon after Bishop Leo's death in 1980, a decision was made to close the seminary despite the objections of leading priests such as the Canadian, Fr. Robert Luckhart, OMI, then director. The closure of Sevaka Sevana only hastened Fr. Mike's decision to put into action his yearning to engage the poor more directly through dialogue, leading him to move to the heart of poverty, Buttala.

It was during his five years at Sevaka Sevana that his aspiration intensified to engage more directly with the poor in a theology of presence. He was entrusted with providing the seminarians with their formal theological preparation. Upon completion of their scholarly grounding in theology, the seminarians were expected to participate in a practicum designed by Fr. Mike. It entailed a contextual experience where they would live and work among the poor. The purpose of the practicum was to deepen their ability to connect scripture to circumstance. The observation of and immersion in the quotidian challenges faced by the poor was meant as a catalyst for reflection and spiritual growth.

The precursor to Fr. Mike's interest in setting up Suba Seth Gedera in the area known as Lower Uva (just south of Bandarawela) was this work among the poor in the Badulla diocese. As he joined the seminarians in their extended residence in the surrounding low-income villages, the idea of committing his life to living among them and working for their upliftment seems to have been formed. As one Christian activist noted,

---

22. Fernando, "Fr. Mike, Prophet and Martyr," para. 1.

He was no armchair critic, but someone who came down to the grassroot level, and totally identified himself with the poor. He chose the region of Lower Uva for his ministry in order to pay compensation to the damages done by Colonial Christianity.[23]

Subsequently, in 1980, he fulfilled this quest by launching his program to work hand-in-hand with the poor. His choice for this undertaking was a hamlet called Alukalavita, in the township of Buttala, a remote, impoverished village area with a long history of poverty and disenfranchisement.

PRESENTING CHRIST TO THE POOR: SIGN AND SYMBOL

In tandem with his deepening convictions about serving the poor, and as an integral part of the second phase of his spiritual transformation, Fr. Mike had begun formulating a theological perspective on presenting Christ as sign and symbol of love and justice among the poor. His vision of being present among the poor, emulating Jesus among the poor, and being present in Christ for the poor emerged in this process.

One of the first steps he took to register his affinity with/for the poor entailed a conscious choice to change his attire from the traditional cassock to the local garb, as a symbolic gesture of identification with them. This move would have arisen from his perceptive understandings of the need to diminish all appearances of difference, beyond the mere goal of establishing rapport with the poor. It was also prompted by his desire to forge an authentic bond of solidarity, with the intention of building a level playing field for communion with the rural poor. He realized that any visible markers of difference would stand in the way of healing the rifts of faith, class, education, etc., which would have interfered in cultivating the common understanding he aspired to achieve. Fr. Mike would have also been sensitive to the indigenous population's perception

> Fr. Michael was entrusted with the pioneering work of formation of students for the priesthood for the missions of the new diocese. So, on weekends the students spent their time in villages and estates sharing the life of the people. Later on, it extended itself to week long, a month long stay in the villages and the students had to learn to subsist on a frugal diet because of a limited budget. Thus they learnt firsthand the problems and tribulations of the people, a necessary pre-requisite for those who wish to serve them.
>
> —Ceylon Today, "Fr. Michael Rodrigo OMI," para. 3.

---

23. Namal, "25 years ago," para. 2.

of the cassock as an alienating symbol of dominance, given the history of colonial affinity with Christianity. For the people of Buttala, the cassock represented the force of colonial power imposed upon them historically, the cultural demoralization and the economic devastation in the wake of colonial forays, long embedded in their historical memory.[24] Fr. Mike was astutely aware of this interpretation, given his understanding of the memory of trauma etched in the psyche of the poor. He would have reasoned that the legitimacy and credibility of his quest for social justice rested on such visible signs of a genuine transformation of consciousness. In effect, it was a visible, corporeal enactment of his identification with the poor of Sri Lanka in a symbolic and literal sense.

Yet another aspect of his turn to indigenous attire that merits consideration is the critique of post-colonial alienation that was an integral part of his quest for social justice. Even though Fr. Mike did not address this topic *per se* in his writing, it was embedded in the passionate critique of economic exploitation, political oppression, and cultural domination he had been immersed in. We may thus surmise that he was familiar with and in agreement with post-colonial theorizing.[25] Unlike the theoretical ambit of post-colonial studies, however, Fr. Mike proposed spiritual renewal as the avenue to social justice. Yet, it was not a passive engagement in spiritual renewal that he was referring to—it was an active engagement in redressing historical injustices *together* with the poor, in a manner that would render the poor as subjects of their destiny (not as objects of paternalistic benevolence). In the language of human rights conventions, he was unique in possessing the foresight to support their *rights claims* and pave the way for their self-reliance. The author recalls conversations with Fr. Mike in 1987 at SSG where he explicated such an empowering vision for the poor.

Moreover, in light of the persistent socioeconomic disparities between urban and rural populations, and the markers of class identity evident in Western garb, he would have striven to erase as far as possible any visible sources of social distance. Although this decision was received with less than enthusiasm by the church hierarchy, it was widely admired by the Oblate congregation, not only for the courage that it embodied, but also for its symbolic significance in enacting service for the poor. While many in the

---

24. For example, as a result of the complete destruction of the region's irrigation infrastructure by the British colonial authorities in 1818, in response to the local rebellion mobilized to protest British rule.

25. See for example, Rodrigo, "Example of Village Dialogue."

church hierarchy were baffled by this turn, those who grasped its deeper implications marveled at his courage.

From the vantage point of the rural poor of Buttala, it was an action that dissipated the social distance between them and Fr. Mike, given that he represented another faith, and whose education and class position was in marked contrast to theirs. More powerfully, it communicated a tacit recognition of their worth, the value of their cultural and social location—certainly a source of inherent empowerment. It was one of many steps in Fr. Mike's journey for justice that suspended social, class, and faith affiliations and paved the way for a commonality of purpose with the poor.

For Fr. Mike, the significance attributed to adopting local/native attire (i.e., the *sarong* and *banion*[26] instead of the priestly cassock) rested in his interpretation of indigenization in Christ's message. Such a choice of donning indigenous attire was also integral to his intention to render pride of place to local culture and a concern with decolonizing the disempowered rural masses. It entailed a corporeal manifestation of the particular spiritual transformation he was undergoing. It was also a visible sign of the shifts in his convictions about his mission, and of the cataclysmic evolution in understanding his call that he would have experienced in the deepest recesses of his being. Ultimately, it also signified a point of departure, a mile-post of no return, signaling his abandonment of middle-class comforts as he moved closer to the poor, and a confirmation of his pledge to serve their cause of redemption and healing. In effect, it represented a true embodiment of the Poor Jesus concept.

---

26. The term "banyan" is also commonly used across the Indian Subcontinent to refer to what is known as a T-shirt elsewhere in the world.

3

Bridge of Faith
Dialogue, Dialogy, and Key Theological Perspectives

> My father hailed from a Buddhist/Methodist milieu in the south of Sri Lanka and my closest relations are from Buddhism and Methodism, and so wishing to be an ecumenist, I started Buddhist-Christian dialogue very early.
>
> —Rodrigo, quoted in Balasuriya, "Fr. Michael Rodrigo OMI," 4.

ACROSS THE CHRISTIAN COMMUNITY in Sri Lanka, among lay and ordained groups, Fr. Mike is recognized as a brilliant theologian[1] who espoused a radically novel ecumenical vision and an interfaith mission. He has been acclaimed as "one of the luminaries of the seminary" by leading Asian theologians such as Fr. Aloysius (Aloy) Pieris (personal interview with the author, July 29, 2016). Among the major theological conceptualizations Fr. Mike advanced was theorizing around a dialogue between Buddhist and Christian communities. Subsequently, he put this concept into practice through a methodology he developed called Dialogue in Action (see page 45). As an ecumenist, he saw the potential of collaborative efforts across the Christian church, as well as with other faiths, especially in the quest for social justice. A statement in his 1973 PhD thesis captures his views on this

> Dialogue with Other Living Faiths draws within its praxis, common work for justice and equity, which alone makes for peace. It would take the forming of people's community or Communities rather than Basic Christian Communities which may tend to be one sided and more sacramentalizing than totalizing.
>
> —Rodrigo, "Moral Passover," 118.

---

1. This is attested to in the comments of many Oblate priests, Fr. Aloysius Pieris, a leading theologian of the Jesuit Order, representatives of the Anglican Church, and Buddhist leaders alike.

topic (see quotation in box on previous page). Pope Francis's recent affirmation of ecumenism, as it was emphasized in the directives of Vatican II, illustrates the current valence of Fr. Mike's ecumenical vision.

> At the Second Vatican Council, the Catholic Church declared her deep and abiding respect for other religions. She stated that she 'rejects nothing of what is true and holy in these religions. She has a high regard for their manner of life and conduct, their precepts and doctrines' (Nostra Aetate, 2). For my part, I wish to reaffirm the Church's sincere respect for you, your traditions and beliefs.[2]

As his conceptualizations evolved, Fr. Mike began developing a novel understanding of Vatican II edicts, which became the core of his theological formulations. Vatican II had put forward a declaration on the importance of winning people over to the church through outreach and accommodation of local cultural contexts. Fr. Mike relied on this as a springboard to articulate how such an indigenous adaptation of the teachings of Christ could in fact serve as a vehicle for interfaith understanding. Also central to Fr. Mike's theological advances were the concepts of selflessness and self-sacrifice (the focus of his second PhD), compassion as the root of sacrifice, and justice for the poor. These perspectives were influenced by his intimate knowledge of Buddhism (the subject of his first PhD). This chapter delves into how he developed these formulations and most importantly, how he put them to practice.

INDIGENIZATION OF THE GOSPEL

Prior to the embrace of Christianity by the Roman Empire (circa fourth century), there was a common understanding that Christianity must accommodate itself to local cultures and lingua. This practice was more common among the Eastern Orthodox churches than those of Western Europe where Latin remained the ecclesiastical language, regrettably unintelligible to large segments of the uneducated. In the Eastern churches,

> For Fr. Mike, indigenization was not simply adaptation of certain aspects of local art, decorations, vestments, and liturgy; instead, it was a question of incarnating the Christian teaching in the lives of the people. True indigenization involves taking the liberational content of the Gospel into the hearts of the poor masses.
>
> —Namal, "25 Years Ago," para. 3.

---

2. Francis, "Pope: We Must Be Forthright," para. 3.

however, the liturgy was translated into local vernacular languages, allowing the population at large to worship in their own languages. As the Jesuit missionary movement came into being in the sixteenth century, there was a call to accommodate Christianity to the Chinese and Indian cultures.

> He believed in theologizing from below, rather than theologizing from above. We tend to take a set of dogmas and apply them to the context of the people (Descending theology). By contrast, Fr. Mike started from below. He was keen to get an intimate understanding of people's experience at the grass roots. He analyzed it, asking why people have to go through so much suffering. He searched for the roots of injustice. Then he reflected on them in the light of the Word of God and moved to action. He chose small actions at local level to better the situation of the people. He often said, "Think global and act local."
>
> — Sr. Winifreda Wasalathanthrige, personal communication, November 16, 2016.

Vatican II is acknowledged as the hallmark moment when indigenization of the gospel and faith practice was officially sanctioned by the Catholic Church. Subsequently, as the force of indigenization gathered momentum on many fronts during the 1970s (in a climate of budding nationalist fervor in the post-colonial era and with struggles for national sovereignty and autonomy growing around the world), the church as an institution became increasingly aware of the importance of indigenization, including of the gospel and its message. In Sri Lanka, this prompted the translation of English hymns to Sinhala (and to some extent Tamil), as well as a moment when hymns came to be composed in Sinhala. This type of cultural grounding lent itself to the realization of yet another call of Vatican II—contextualization—the process of enlivening the faith mission through the lens of its own cultural and historical setting. Fr. Mike was a perspicacious advocate for such an approach in the Catholic Church of Sri Lanka. His theological perspectives advanced the necessity of this kind of localization. As one of his former students, Fr. Oswald Firth, OMI, clarifies,

> He tried to make the church visible, tangible, and infinitely accessible to the people. He was searching for a way to adapt theology to the people and their beliefs. He had undergone a profound shift in this thinking as a result of Vatican II—it was based on a break with the hierarchical clerical tradition to a Kingdom centered approach—to bring God to the people, rather than vice versa.[3]

In Fr. Mike's view, such an approach was not only essential for the spread of Christian tenets, but also in embracing others into the fold of Christianity. Yet, his fundamental objective was not to seek conversions *per*

3. Firth, personal interview, July 2016.

se, but rather to offer Christ's message and living spirit as a source of healing and empowerment. He visualized this process occurring by his witnessing Christ to the poor. According to Fr. Oswald Firth,

> He was keen to present Jesus as one who was among the people, the poor, worked with them, and supported them. His whole Christology was not of Jesus in the clouds, but a Christ who was a living, suffering presence.[4]

The device or vehicle that he envisioned as the entry point for such witnessing was a *dialogue*—a Buddhist-Christian Dialogue—discussed in the section below.

History of Interfaith Dialogue in Sri Lanka

Rev. Lynn de Silva is credited as being the individual who reenergized interfaith, especially Buddhist-Christian dialogue in Sri Lanka with the launching of one of the first journals on the topic in 1961 and the founding of the Ecumenical Institute for Study and Dialogue (EISD) in 1962. Prior to that, the record of interfaith exchange in Sri Lanka had been acrimonious at best, dating back to the famous Panadura Debates of 1873, which was an attempt by the Buddhist leaders of the day to restore the dignity of Buddhism, given the discredit to which it had been subjected under colonial rule.

BUDDHIST-CHRISTIAN DIALOGUE

Fr. Mike is considered a pioneer in the notion and practice of Buddhist-Christian dialogue. The main distinguishing characteristic of the latter was that it was not merely an interfaith dialogue *per se*, but rather one that was an *engagement* with the Buddhist poor. He articulated this particular emphasis on engaging with the poor through his concept of the dialogue of life, drawing upon insights gained through his first-hand exchanges with the poor. As such, Fr. Mike's work among the poor in Buttala did not remain solely at the level of a dialogue—in the sense of dialogue as a mere conversational exchange on faith beliefs and practices. It was a concrete *engagement* with the lives and livelihood struggles of the poor, intended to culminate in a *transformative* interconnection and alliance of equals, grounded in his conviction of the inherent dignity of the poor. It can only be understood as an actualization of dialogue—a living act of belief in practice for the purpose of human liberation, spiritual and otherwise (e.g., from the bonds of economic exploitation and social oppression). To Fr. Mike, this was the fundamental

4. Ibid.

charge of Christianity: to serve as a spiritually liberative force. As one of his former students, Brother Jude Lal Fernando noted,

> Fr. Mike used to say very often, "for us Christians, conversion is an hourly, daily affair with God, not something left to Buddhists, Hindus, Muslims and Marxists and others, and it is specially meant for Christians to see if they, as salt are sapid; as light enlighten; as leaven make pare bread to foster and feed life."[5]

In general, a dialogue is understood as a process that aims for a common goal of reaching mutual understanding, beyond a mere verbal exchange. Standard dictionary definitions for dialogue denote its meaning as an exchange of ideas or opinions on a particular issue, with a view to reaching an amicable agreement or settlement. Such definitions are wholly inadequate to fully capture Fr. Mike's interpretation of "dialogue," especially in terms of his deeper intentions in formulating the notion or device of a Buddhist-Christian dialogue. His conceptualization of the latter included a notion he referred to as "dialogue in action," to signify the efforts to arrive at a common understanding on the course of action to be taken on pressing social issues, illuminated through core theological beliefs across diverse faiths. Therefore, in Fr. Mike's vision, the Buddhist-Christian dialogue was not an engagement that rested solely at the level of a verbal exchange. It was instead a living, active engagement that far surpassed the boundaries of dialogue in the sense of a verbal exchange alone. It was a critical launching pad for a deeper and more action-oriented *praxis* of community and common purpose for uplifting and empowering the poor, which he understood as Christ's call to all of humanity.

From all available accounts, it appears that he began contemplating how to devise a conceptual tool to bridge the understanding between Buddhist and Christian communities around the early 1960s. While he was cognizant of the historical divide between the Buddhist and Christian communities in Sri Lanka,

---

The Panadura Debates: Buddhist Challenge to Christianity

During the late 1800s, as a tide of repressive sentiments grew against Buddhism, a national challenge arose from a Buddhist monk from Galle, Ven. Migettuwatte Gunananda Thero. Through a series of debates with Christian clergy, he staged an eloquent defense of Buddhism and the right for native faith practice. Culminating in a two-day public exchange, the Panadura Debates have tremendous social and historical significance in reestablishing the identity and pride of Sinhala Buddhists.

---

5. Fernando, "Fr. Michael Rodrigo and His Contribution," 107.

at least on matters of faith,[6] his extensive knowledge of Christian scripture and Buddhist philosophy would have convinced Fr. Mike that, in fact, there was a common truth between the two faith belief systems. The question in his mind then would have been how best to bridge the two, through theological conceptualizations as well as from a pragmatic perspective. He would have also drawn inspiration from the emerging Christian thought at the time in Sri Lanka (then known as Ceylon), which was in and of itself partly energized by the directives of Vatican II (see below) about contextualizing theology to the cultural milieu. Together with Methodist minister, Lynn de Silva, Fr. Mike, and other progressive contemporaries (i.e., Fr. Aloy Pieris, Fr. Tissa Balasuriya, and Fr. Paul Caspersz) focused on theological ideas that would enhance the relevance and credibility of Christianity in a country steeped in Buddhist history and culture, where the majority population practiced Buddhism.

> Christians in a dialogical experience in a totally non-Christian milieu proclaim Jesus by witness, for he never worked for Himself but for the ongoing reign of God. God himself in the fullness of time sent his Incarnate Son into the world to free human persons from every form of slavery—to which they were subject by reason of sin and human egoism. Jesus' first preaching was to proclaim the liberation of the oppressed.
>
> —Rodrigo, quoted in Fernando, *Harvest Dreams*, 56.

Moreover, in light of the discordant history of the two faiths, exposed in the Panadura Debates (see box on previous page), it is likely that Fr. Mike recognized the importance of bringing about greater understanding between the two communities. As an erudite scholar, he was quite knowledgeable of the history of Buddhist repression at the hands of colonial powers and Christian missionaries in Sri Lanka during the 1800s and its lingering aftereffects in the rural periphery. His acute awareness of the historical injustices endured by the Buddhist population, often at the hands of Christian powers, would have driven his quest for reconciling the centuries-old misgivings and misunderstandings between the Buddhist and Christian communities of Sri Lanka. In addition, his first-hand observations of the plight of poverty stricken rural Buddhist masses in the course of his excursions into the rural areas of Uva[7] during his teaching years at the Ampitiya seminary would have deepened his desire to develop this line of thinking.

6. It should be noted that despite the adherence to diverse faith traditions, intermarriage is quite common in Sri Lanka, although it often entailed one spouse choosing to convert. At the same time, there are many examples of marriages that thrived in an environment of mutual accommodation (i.e., in the absence of a choice conversion).

7. Uva is the southeastern province of the island nation of Sri Lanka, and includes two

Furthermore, as a person with a bent for being a social critic, he would have also observed not only the (perceived) gaps in faith perceptions, intentions and aspirations, but also the deep class divide in Sri Lanka, especially during the colonial and post-colonial era, where the Christian elite tended to dominate the social and economic life of the nation. Despairing at what he saw around him, he would have felt compelled to right those historical wrongs, starting by establishing common ground between the two communities as a path to peace and social justice. Therein lay the foundations of his vision to forge an enduring bridge between the two communities.

The most important contribution that Fr. Mike made in this regard is his effort to elucidate the compelling parallels between the basic tenets of Christianity and Buddhism, contrary to the commonly held belief at the time that the two faith traditions were in stark contrast to each other. Interestingly enough, he approached it from the perspective of the Buddhists as the starting point and not the other way around. This is evident in the formulation of the concept with Buddhism as the first noun followed by Christian. In other words, he was keen to reach out to the Buddhist community on their own terms, not on the basis of a Christian standpoint, a formidable challenge in and of itself, as scholars of religion and theology have hence elaborated. As his thinking evolved, he articulated these parallels in his second doctoral thesis, "The Moral Passover: From Self to Selflessness in Christianity and the Living Faiths of Asia," completed in 1973 at the Institut Catholique in Paris, France.

CHALLENGES INHERENT IN INTERFAITH DIALOGUE

Religious scholars and theologians who have written about and analyzed the notion and practice of interfaith dialogue have consistently identified the challenges it represents. One forbidding starting point has been the tendency to deem one's faith as superior, and the other as inferior. This divide has led some scholars to consider it a virtually unattainable task, declared as the "near impossibility of achieving a true dialogue."[8] Adherence to the convic-

---

districts, Badulla and Moneragala, both known as the poverty pockets of the country. It is a province of mythical and cultural importance, with several landmarks associated with the mythical king Ravana and several ancient temples, one of which, the Mahiyangana Raja Maha Vihara is recognized as a place visited by the Lord Buddha. Uva is home to some spectacular natural features: the world famous Dunhinda, Diyaluma and Ravana Ella waterfalls, two national parks (Gal Oya and Yala), and two mountain ranges offering breathtaking views all the way to the Indian Ocean: Haputale and Namunakula.

8. Cornille, *Impossibility*, 4.

tions of one's own faith is thought to represent a significant, if not impenetrable barrier to the objective of dialogue, which aims for insights and understanding of the other's perspectives. In other words, scholars addressing this topic have argued that interreligious dialogue continues to represent an indomitable challenge for most religious traditions.

> **Conditions Necessary for Interreligious Dialogue**
> - Doctrinal or epistemic humility
> - Commitment to a particular religious tradition
> - Interconnection for meaningful conversation
> - Empathy as a presupposition to understanding the other tradition
> - Hospitality to the authentic truth of the other religious tradition
>
> —Cornille, *Impossibility*, 4–5.

Cornille, for example, presents several conditions amenable to engaging in genuine interreligious understanding, emphasizing the difficulty of all such conditions being met by any single individual or religious tradition. As shown above, the conditions identified by Cornille represent a host of near-impossible challenges that are not easily overcome. The first of these, epistemic humility, suggests the need for deep reflection on the epistemic principles of one's faith along with the willingness to recognize the epistemic offerings of the other faith tradition. It calls for a recognition of the other faith as one that could offer spiritual insights that may augment or enrich one's own faith beliefs.

The second condition, that of remaining committed to one's particular tradition while engaging with another is posited as a challenge based on the premise that accommodating both represents a cognitive conundrum. According to Cornille, interreligious dialogue

> does presuppose commitment to a particular worldview and belief system and a willingness to attest to its truth and validity in dialogue with other worldviews and belief systems.[9]

The challenge in this regard is the willingness to be open to the alternative routes and conceptualizations of truth, love, grace, mercy, and charity offered by another tradition.

The third condition, interconnection for a meaningful conversation, is considered a challenge because of the preestablished barriers that are

---

9. Ibid., 59.

likely to deter a significant exchange. The fourth condition, empathy for the tenets and practices of another faith tradition, is put forward as a serious challenge, given that it calls for a certain receptivity of heart and mind sufficient to accept and embrace divergent tenets and practices. The final condition, hospitality, is considered a challenge because it calls for a rare openness to the beliefs and traditions of another faith, regardless of how much they may diverge from one's own.

Cornille also identifies yet another foundational challenge inherent to the quest of interfaith dialogue—the cultural dilemma of Christian engagement—the suspicion surrounding Christian work among the poor and in various corners of the world as a "covert form of proselytizing."[10] Indeed, the tacit if not outright resistance by indigenous communities in many places around the world to missionary incursions is based on the apprehension about such a covert if not explicit agenda. Therein lies the enormity of the task that Fr. Mike initiated and dedicated himself to. It is in the context of such daunting challenges that Fr. Mike initiated the formulation of a dialogue with the Buddhist communities of Sri Lanka. Evidence from the work he accomplished among the Buddhist poor of the remote rural area known as Buttala, in Sri Lanka, attests to the ways in which he overcame these challenges and succeeded in achieving an active praxis of interfaith dialogue.

FUNDAMENTALS OF THE BRIDGE OF FAITH

The starting point of Fr. Mike's conceptualization of a Buddhist-Christian dialogue was his deep conviction about the wisdom and insights offered by Buddhism as a philosophy. This alone is indicative of the fact that he was not impeded by the challenges outlined by Cornille. His long-term study of Buddhism equipped him with an extensive knowledge base of Buddhist soteriology. That expertise enabled him to elucidate what he deemed as the indisputable parallels between Buddhist and Christian thought and tenets, analyzed in detail in his second doctoral thesis. He also assumed a stance of pronounced epistemic humility in formulating his concept of a bridge of faith between Buddhism and Christianity, rooted in his belief that humility was a cornerstone of Christ's message and a central tenet of Christianity. He was therefore convinced that humility was the starting point in achieving oneness with Christ and that interfaith dialogue had to be conducted through a comportment of humility, premised in love-agape.

10. Ibid., 7.

In this manner, Fr. Mike's position on interfaith dialogue met the first challenging condition identified by Cornille:

> It is through humility and love that one is able to truly understand the other and empathize with his or her experiences and feelings.... Humility facilitates understanding through love of the other.[11]

The second condition identified as a challenge by Cornille—the rootedness in a commitment to a particular religious tradition while "in dialogue with other worldviews and belief systems"—was met by Fr. Mike in a unique way. Throughout his life, he had not only been exposed to Buddhist beliefs and practices, but had participated in the latter to varying degrees by virtue of his enduring bonds with extended family members. Yet, he remained firmly anchored in the Christian belief of Christ as the route to salvation. Although he adhered to a belief in the essential truth of Christianity and Christ's message of mercy, grace, and love as the ultimate redeeming possibility for humanity, he had grown up observing parallel notions in Buddhism in the world around him, embodied in the central tenets of Buddhism": *Karuna*, *Metta*, *Mudita*, *Upekha*, and *Ahimsa*.[12] By analyzing these parallel tenets in both faith traditions, Fr. Mike understood that the end goal of dialogue was not necessarily conversion. Instead, his position was that conversion was the result of divine intervention. His main purpose in advancing the idea of accommodating a parallel belief system was to pave the way for peaceful coexistence, which he believed to be the ultimate purpose of all faiths. In this way, Fr. Mike fulfilled yet another presupposition of interreligious dialogue, equality, which Cornille argues,

> refers to the equal personal dignity of the parties in dialogue, not to doctrinal content, not even less to the position of Jesus Christ—who is God himself made man.[13]

---

11. Cornille, *Many Mansions*, 24.

12. Buddhist doctrine sets out four divine states, also known as the four "Brahma Viharas" (highest or divine emotions). These are: *Metta* (loving kindness), *Karuna* (compassion), *Mudita* (sympathetic joy in the success of others), and *Upekha* (equanimity). See Nyanatiloka, *Buddhist Dictionary*, 37. I am grateful to Fr. Claude Perera for providing this clarification, as part of the detailed review he undertook of this manuscript, which included both editorial and substantive guidance. Although it is not part of the four divine states, *Ahimsa* (nonviolence) has been considered the highest virtue in the main religious traditions of the subcontinent of India, including Buddhism, Hinduism, and Jainism, for three thousand years.

13. Cornille, *Impossibility*, 88–89.

RETURN TO SOURCE: COMPASSION AS THE FOUNDATION OF BUDDHIST-CHRISTIAN DIALOGUE

Most scholarly accounts of interfaith dialogue have analyzed its premises, aims, and challenges. Yet, to date, none have touched upon the germinal role of compassion as the source of inspiration for engaging in such an exchange. The essence of compassion is difficult to capture through an analytical lens. Compassion rests in the realm of spirit and heart. It defies scholarly dissection. It is without formula. Compassion dwells in the depths of a heart furiously stirred by the suffering of others, as Fr. Mike's life journey so palpably exemplified. There is no doubt that Fr. Mike's work among the poor of Sri Lanka was rooted in a deep compassion for the grueling poverty they endured on a daily basis, as well as over time—their pervasive marginality and persistent social and economic disempowerment. Acutely cognizant of the current realities they confronted, his engagement through the vehicle of Buddhist-Christian dialogue was not through a fixed or fossilized intellectual stance on doctrinal equality, or an academic quest for common ground. Instead, it was inspired by the kind of active empathy, the wellspring of compassion that Christ himself embodied. Compassion or its equivalent *Metta* in Buddhism, is one of the concepts that Fr. Mike meditated on, discussed extensively in his second PhD thesis, and served as the entry point for his work in Alukalavita village, Buttala.

The quintessence of compassion is the interphase of empathy (the human ability to feel and understand the emotional state and felt experiences of another person) and altruism (exhibitions of selfless behavior), where we are moved enough to engage in actions that relieve another's suffering. Compassion thus bridges two aspects: human emotions (the response of the heart) and the cognitive faculties (the mental response). Research undertaken by a handful of scientists point to the biological basis of compassion, suggesting its evolutionary significance, in terms of the survival of humanity. This body of research alludes to the importance of nurture for human survival, not only the nurture of our offspring during their early, vulnerable years, but also for our continuity in connection to others. These scientists thus argue that compassion can in fact be vital to the survival of all of humanity. Fr. Mike embodied all aspects of this notion of compassion, which served as a heart compass[14] directing his journey for justice.

14. Typically, right living is attributable to a strong moral compass, which denotes the faculty of judgement in assessing right from wrong. Yet, given that compassion rests more on a quality of heart beyond intellectual reasoning, I have refrained from using the

Fr. Mike's engagement with and struggle to uplift the impoverished communities of Buttala showed the incredible depth of compassion he possessed. It also entailed a form of self-sacrifice that approximated Christ's divine sacrifice at the cross. Indeed, Fr. Mike's quest was to model his faith journey in complete devotion to Christ's summons to serve the poor. Although his decision to embark on that journey departed to some extent from the mandate of the church as an institution, he hastened to respond to the call of his heart—the extraordinary compassion that welled up in him upon witnessing the plight of the poor. Compassion was the fire that ignited his soul to action and that sparked his fervor to ameliorate the injuries of poverty and injustice, despite the risk to life and limb.

> The importance of Fr. Mike lies not so much in his expertise of Buddhism, but in his dedication to the cause of the poor. . . . Coming from the high class society in Colombo, he sacrificed many things for the sake of the noble cause of the poor masses for whom he had made a preferential option.
>
> —Namal, "25 Years Ago," para. 3.

DIALOGUE IN ACTION: AVENUE TO SOCIAL JUSTICE

The Pontifical Council for Interreligious Dialogue and the Congregation for the Evangelization of Peoples has identified four facets of interreligious dialogue: life, action, theological exchange, and religious experience (see the Dialogue and Proclamation no. 42).

According to Lowe, the dialogue of life refers to "common living as good neighbor," dialogue in action refers to "collaboration for development and liberation," dialogue of theological exchange entails "understanding of different religious heritage," and dialogue of religious experience calls for "sharing of spiritual riches."[15] Fr. Mike chose to focus primarily on the dialogue of action because of his inherent conviction about the dire need for active engagement in social justice. Hence, in his view, engagement in dialogue of action was the route to transformative witnessing of Christ beyond the mere exchange of words or ideas. As clarified in his second doctoral thesis, "But Christ is not only the Word (Logos). He is the Doing Word

---

term moral compass in my analysis of the extraordinary compassion that Fr. Mike was endowed with.

15. Lowe, "Word-Crucified in the Theology," 210.

(Dabar, in Aramaic, or the *Word in Action*). Men can come to Him through the *action* of the Word, or through the *Word* acting on them, and in them."[16]

Fourteen years after articulating the above in his 1973 doctoral thesis, Fr. Mike expounded further on the notion of *dabar* by linking it to the work he had undertaken in Buttala among the poor.

> Jesus is Word of God as doing-word, the Verb of God (dabar in Aramaic). It is the source of orthodoxy and orthopraxis, of Christian saying and doing, or promise and fulfilment. Our presence must speak to all, as an eloquent presence, to point to the eternal Word.[17]

This aspect of enacting Christ's presence in action has been elaborated by the leading Asian theologian today, Fr. Mike's close friend and colleague Fr. Aloy Pieris in his extensive writing on this theme.[18] As clarified by Lowe,

> However, according to Pieris, Jesus is the Word of God in the sense of dabar, event-Word. Jesus Christ as the event-Word is not merely a speech that displays authoritative knowledge, but an utterance that creates and transforms. In the dabar model it is the execution of the Word that brings understanding of the Word. For Pieris, in a dabar pattern of theology knowledge comes from love and fidelity (1 John 4:8, 20). It is the fidelity to the Covenant of Love that is Jesus Christ, the Word-Crucified himself. It is that knowledge or understanding which is salvific. Hence, the knowledge in the dabar model calls for an encounter with the One who is our Love and our Salvation and, a commitment to his mission of love rather than mere logical inference as in the logos model.[19]

More significantly, this kind of action was interpreted by Fr. Mike not merely as restorative action, but as *transformative* action.

> It is not enough for the Christian to give a cup of cold water in the name of Christ, today. To be true to the truth, he must politically agitate to set up a waterworks, and this is a matter of justice.[20]

In sum, Fr. Mike firmly believed that the power of a wider ecumenical dialogue derived from its ultimate purpose—to bring about social justice.

---

16. Rodrigo, "Moral Passover," 143.
17. Rodrigo, "Hope of Liberation," 191.
18. See Pieris, "Christ Beyond Dogma."
19. Lowe, "Word-Crucified," 91.
20. Rodrigo, "Moral Passover," 144.

> Dialogue with Other Living Faiths draws within its praxis, common work for justice and equity, which alone makes for peace. It would take in the forming of people's Community or Human Communities rather than Basic Christian Communities which may tend to be one-sided and more sacramentalizing than totalizing.[21]

This is yet another aspect of interfaith dialogue that merits further analysis, given the scarcity of living examples of individuals who have embarked on such an engagement. In sum, for Fr. Mike, the Buddhist-Christian Dialogue was an avenue for attaining a larger goal: an immersion in the experiential dimension of poverty endured by those at the margins of society, of embracing their suffering, and advocating for their rights and dignity. His vision of this process is articulated in a 1987 paper presented at the Christian Conference of Asia, Hong Kong:

> Then respect for human dignity becomes the creating of a society based on people's needs. If we are committed to them, involved with them and among them, rather than working *for* them, the very process of decision-making with them will become a transforming presence. We—the Jesus community—will not be mere catalyst, for in the process of mutual presence, the people will be "doing the truth in love," and that transforms us both, when people become the architects of their own destiny.[22]

This perspective is aligned with the cause for social justice that Jesus Christ himself took up during his earthly life, certainly a radical challenge to the power exercised by the political and religious authorities of his time, a vociferous decrying of the material and spiritual oppression he witnessed.

LIVING ENACTMENT OF LIBERATION THEOLOGY

Fr. Mike's living out his convictions about liberating the poor would have also been influenced by liberation theology, which gained ground during the early 1970s as a contextualized theology to address the mass destitution observable in many developing countries. In many of his writings, Fr. Mike echoed and elucidated the idea of a preferential option for the poor, a core notion of liberation theology and one that has also been elaborated upon by other key Sri Lankan theologians, including Fr. Paul Caspersz, and especially Fr. Aloy

---

21. Ibid., 118.
22. Rodrigo, "Hope of Liberation," 193. Author's emphasis.

Pieris.[23] This body of theological beliefs would have struck a resonating chord with Fr. Mike's understanding of poverty as an inherent contradiction if not a violation of the divine will of justice and equality.

Departing to some extent from the focus on the liturgy for the purpose of salvation from sin (i.e., people flocking to the gospel), liberation theology advocated for the *gospel going to the people*, as a corrective to the indignities and injustices of poverty. There was thus a political "agenda" embedded in liberation theology—a mission to liberate the downtrodden from their concrete experiences of poverty, as a core directive of Christianity. While some contend that Jesus's mission was solely focused on the spiritual welfare of humanity, liberation theologians argued that the church had an obligation to be a voice for the poor, to serve the poor, to uplift them and immerse itself in the cause of social justice by challenging the very structures of oppression. Addressing the social structures and practices at the root of the oppressive conditions of poverty was considered to be an intrinsic part of this call. Liberation theology thus questioned the source of poverty, the roots of inequity and did not accept poverty as a *prima facie* given. Peruvian theologian Gustavo Gutierrez, credited with articulating the first ideas of what came to be known as liberation theology in 1968 as an "option for the poor" provides a further clarification on the social production of poverty:

> The poor are a by-product of the system in which we live and for which we are responsible. They are marginalized by our social and cultural world. They are the oppressed, exploited proletariat, robbed of the fruit of their labor and despoiled of their humanity.[24]

During the 1970s and 1980s, the ideas of liberation theology were being debated and reflected upon by many Christian leaders in Sri Lanka, such as Fr. Tissa Balasuriya, Fr. Paul Caspersz, and others. However, it is safe to say that the notion of *praxis* and its enactment that is at the core of liberation theology was catapulted onto the center of the spiritual stage of Sri Lanka through Fr. Mike's work in Buttala and his theological advances on witnessing to the poor. Fr. Mike understood human liberation as rooted in the gospel's message about restoring the dignity of the human being created in the image of God, which included liberation from the intersectional oppressions of political persecution, economic disenfranchisement, racial/

---

23. See for example, Pieris, *Asian Theology*.
24. Guitierrez, *Power of the Poor*, 44.

ethnic discrimination, social marginality, and cultural suppression. He bemoaned the social and economic inequities inherent in Sri Lankan society and found the systemic forces and institutional mechanisms that perpetuated these inequities abhorrent. The contrasting emphasis on spiritual "poverty" and material poverty embedded in liberation theology did not represent a conundrum for Fr. Mike. He saw them as integrally linked because of his immersion in the notion of divine love for the poor. Fr. Mike's work in Buttala thus represented a discernible enactment of the tenets of liberation theology.

The Brazilian scholar Leonardo Boff[25] argues that the mechanisms of impoverishment and exploitation that reproduce poverty are perceived as fundamental injustices in liberation theology. The challenge then, for the adherents of liberation theology, was to uncover the forces of history and structures in society that lent themselves to the injustice of poverty. One of the leading proponents of liberation theology, Paolo Freire, a Brazilian political philosopher, had coined the term "conscientization" for the basic process that could excavate these forces, one which Fr. Mike had introduced to the seminarians at Ampitiya and Sevaka Sevana.

According to Freire, conscientization is,

> the process in which men, not as recipients, but as knowing subjects, achieve a deepening awareness both of the socio-cultural reality which shapes their lives and their capacity to transform that reality.[26]

We may thus understand conscientization as a process that entailed an interrogation of the structural impediments that keep the poor entrenched in poverty. Fr. Mike guided the young seminarians in such a process of conscientization not only in the classroom where they relied on the tools of social analysis to uncover the underlying mechanisms involved in impoverization, but also by witnessing it around them, in the adjoining rural areas where they encountered abject poverty face to face. These exercises were designed to deepen their consciousness of poverty and to stir in them a desire to engage in acts of social justice. All the while, however, it appears, he was yearning for something more, beyond the confines of academia, to confront the systemic injustice of poverty head on, and to dive deeply in to a redemptive process of social justice.

---

25. Boff, *Faith on the Edge*.
26. Schubeck, *Liberation Ethics*, 46 note 41.

FROM DIALOGUE TO A TRANSFORMATIVE DIALOGY: THE FIFTH WAY

In the last few months of his life, Fr. Mike seems to have been immersed in an even deeper contemplation about religion, theology, and dialogue as a way to bridge faith traditions, and as a route to social justice. These ideas were put forward in papers he presented at two events: an interreligious conference at Berkeley, California, in 1987, and the Christian Conference of Asia (also convened in 1987) in Hong Kong. As discussed above, he advanced the notion of theology as a practice that served a "transforming presence of the Word in the world," arguing for a deep engagement *with* the poor, rather than *for* the poor. He also reflected on how such a "doing theology" goes beyond a mere dialogue toward a collective effort to *transform* "the oppressive and exploitative economic, social, political, cultural structures,"[27] instead of simply *reforming* the latter.

> Fr. Mike had a passionate love for Christ. His focus was on Christ who moved with people. He often used the word *ochlos* in Greek, which means crowds. He saw Christ moving with the people and being compassionate towards them.
>
> — Sr. Winifreda Wasalathanthri, personal communication, November 16, 2016

He emphasized the role of service as the actualization of faith, a key aspect of Jesus' injunctions to humanity. "The act of faith is not in the statement, but in the reality of it."[28] This exhortation to engage in a *praxis* of faith in the spirit of servanthood remains an enduring theme in his theological perspectives, drawing from his exegesis on *kenosis*, the form of servanthood that Christ Jesus assumed (Phil 2:5–8), a self-emptying as part of his embrace of human suffering. Fr. Mike was steeped in this quest of self-emptying, through his hands-on efforts to transform the grim quotidian realities of the poor, together with the poor, and among the poor, as a practice of justice. Ultimately, he served as an authentic witness to "dialogy," the active enactment of theological principles in ushering justice.

---

27. Rodrigo, "Hope of Liberation," 193.
28. Ibid., 210.

4

Faith for Justice
Life and Mission of Suba Seth Gedera

> I came out to the village in July 1980, also as an act of reconciliation and recompense for the damage British Christians did to our peasantry in 1818. When we came here in 1980, it was to a countryside which had suffered the ravages of the 1818 Uva insurrection (or rebellion). The peasants have this in their unconscious memory and the sight of a "Christian-out-for-a-quick conversion-to-his-dangerous-fold" (as monks used to say then) was an eye sore. Healing, reconciling, acceptance of our fault in parading western Christendom (as totally devoid of a sense of the Kingdom). All this is necessary if we are to understand each other on the path of the Dialogue of Life.
>
> —Rodrigo, quoted by Balasuriya, "Fr. Michael Rodrigo OMI," 5.

APPROXIMATELY THREE YEARS PRIOR to his actual relocation in 1980 to the physical heart of poverty in Lower Uva, it appears that Fr. Mike had arrived at a profound understanding about entering the symbolic heart of poverty—Christ's suffering with the poor. His explanation of the specific aims of his work among the poor reveal that presence, witnessing Christ among the poor, and embracing poverty voluntarily were paramount on his mind.

> In July 1977, I asked Bishop Leo whether I could go and live among the Buddhist peasant people of Lower Uva, not on a project of Development, but on a Dialogue and Conscientization effort with the monks and people in a People's Community (PC) rather than in a Basic Christian Community (BCC), based on Populorum Progresso (Development of Peoples), Encyclical of Pope Paul VI, n. 83.[1]

---

1. Rodrigo, "Beginnings of Suba Seth Gedera."

Although it was an area at the social and economic periphery of Sri Lanka, and geographically distant from Christian institutions, this relocation was not a retreat from Christianity for Fr. Mike. It was actually a direct route to the heart of what he perceived as his mission as a Christian. To him, it was the fulfilment of Christ's call for unreserved compassion for humanity: "when I was hungry, you gave me to eat. When I was thirsty, you gave me to drink" (Matt 25:35). It was effectively his unconditional entrance in to Christ's living presence, which he firmly believed to be among the poor, as a source of comfort, redemption, and empowerment for them.

This chapter delves in to several aspects of this phase of Fr. Mike's life, which represented a critical milestone in his journey for justice. It was first of all the culmination of a spiritual metamorphosis that Fr. Mike had been undergoing for several years. Secondly, it was emblematic of his conscious choice of opting for the poor, not only in terms of working for their upliftment, but also in embracing poverty voluntarily—a biblically sanctioned choice according to Fr. Aloy Pieris.[2] Thirdly, as Fr. Mike had reiterated on many an occasion, it was for the purpose of redressing the historical injustices against them.

While the directives of Vatican II would have served as the initial impetus for this choice, his first-hand witnessing of poverty would have no doubt strengthened his resolve to undertake this step. His acute understanding of the very conditions of poverty was gained during the liturgical innovations he had launched as a teacher at the National Seminary in Ampitiya and Sevaka Sevana seminary in Badulla, where he had led the seminarians in excursions to the surrounding village area (discussed in Chapter 3). These excursions had indelibly impressed upon him the precarious conditions under which the poor eked out a living. A heightened

> You do not study the poor or live with the poor for a time, you become poor and die as Jesus did with the poor.
>
> —Rodrigo, in Stuckey, "Dialogue of Life," 81.

consciousness of the deplorable conditions under which the poor in Sri Lanka languished gained through the latter encounter had ignited a moral indignation in the very depths of his soul. The crushing weight of poverty endured by the rural Buddhist farming populations troubled him to no end, prompting his interest in bridging the gulf between the two faiths (Christianity and Buddhism) as a first step toward justice.

2. See Pieris, *God's Reign*.

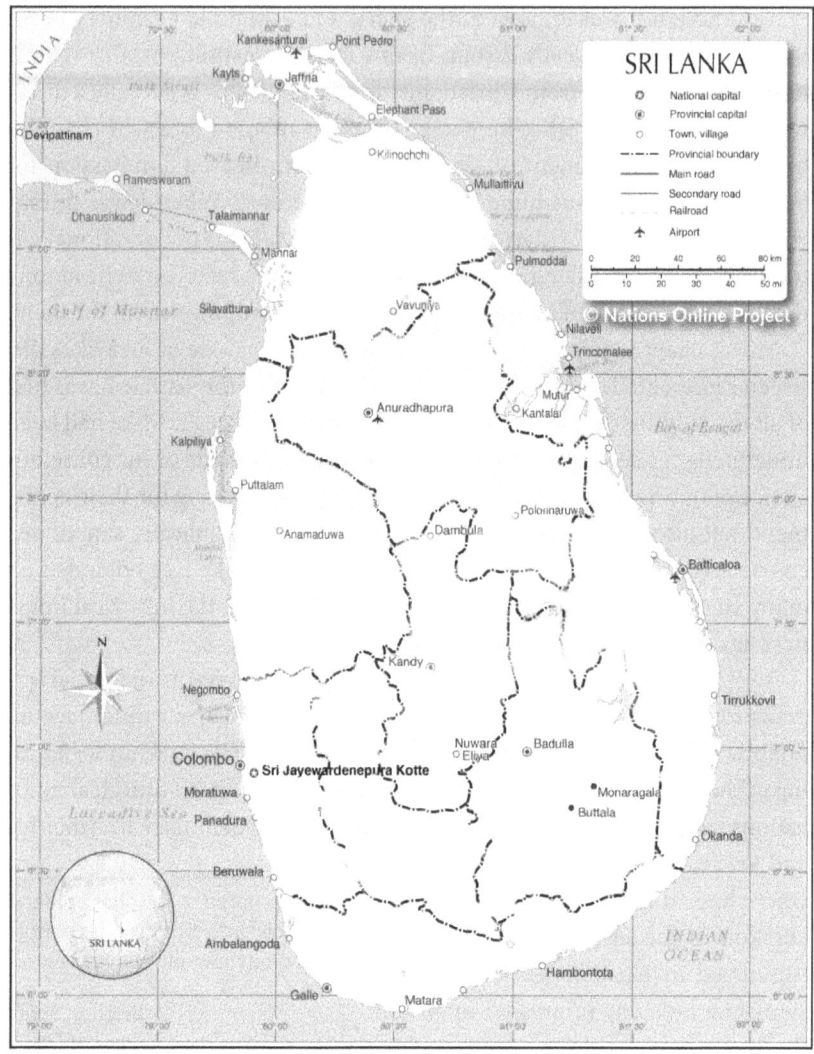

A MORAL PASSOVER: THIRD TRANSFORMATION

The physical move to Buttala, the depths of the wilderness in Sri Lanka's socio-political configuration was emblematic of the third transformation in Fr. Mike's spiritual journey. His decision to shift to an active engagement with the poor by taking up residence in Buttala was based on a conscious choice to devote his life to the poor. Approximately two years into his work at the Sevaka Sevana seminary in the Badulla Diocese (around 1980), Fr. Mike became firmly convinced that he needed to engage with the poor in a more direct manner through a "dialogue of presence," as he referred to it. As he commented to Thomas Stuckey, a theologian who visited Suba Seth Gedera in 1987, entering the world of the poor was not a tempo-

> Lord, we are here to meet you and adore you in the poor peasants of Buttala.
>
> —Rodrigo, prayer (unpublished), 1983, upon receiving a group of Catholic nuns visiting the area for a retreat, recorded by Sr. Winifreda Wasalathanthrige.

rary endeavor. In Fr. Mike's vision, it was not for the purpose of academic edification, or to expand the reach of the church, nor even as a way of "befriending" or "saving" the poor. Far more profoundly, it was for him a total conversion of becoming *one with the poor*—a moral Passover rooted in his understanding of God's identification with the poor, the instrument of salvation. It was also the culminating moment of his identification with the poor.

The option for the poor that Fr. Mike was deeply convinced about was thus embedded in his understanding of the redemptive power of the poor for humanity and for God's purpose with humanity. "The poor will ultimately save the rich and the peasants will save the church of Sri Lanka and give meaning to theological activity," he had proclaimed triumphantly to Thomas Stuckey.³ His vision was that the Christian Church and its representatives are "not called to theologize *about* the poor, or to be a church studying poverty, but to *be* a poor Jesus church, because Jesus is the poor and the poor is Jesus."⁴

Throughout his time at Buttala, Christian theologians such as Stuckey, faith leaders, and practitioners from several Christian communities were hosted by Fr. Mike to "exposures" that were reflective exercises on poverty

> Fr. Michael was a rare exception in that he opted to exercise his priestly duties outside the limits of a parish, a school or other religious institution. He realised that Christianity as conventionally practised in Sri Lanka as well as other parts of the world, lacked the sublime Jesus-vitality that has a benign influence on humanity: this being his macro-interpretation of the second part of what Jesus called the greatest commandment "Love your neighbour as yourself" (Mark 12:29–31, Luke 10:25–28, Matthew 22:34–40). If Christians constitute a very small percentage of Sri Lanka's population, he asked how one could explain the meaningful balance of God's creation.
>
> —Wijeyeratne, "Harvest Dream," para. 4.

---

3. Stuckey, "Dialogue of Life," 80.
4. Author's emphasis.

as an encounter with Jesus. These exposures were called "Poor Jesus seminars" that exposed the participants to the abject hardships endured by the rural poor. The objective of these exposures was to allow the participants to grasp the conditions of poverty in its authentic form, rather than in the comfort of abstract discussions or conferences on poverty convened in star-class hotels in the capital city, Colombo. A visit to Suba Seth Gedera illustrated the stark contrast with the opulence of the latter. An account of such a Poor Jesus Seminar is recounted by Fr. Claude Perera, OMI, who led a group of his Oblate pre-novices to Suba Seth Gedara in June 1986.

> The unbearable heat, swarms of mosquitos, bathing in the muddy water of the nearly dry Karawila Kanaththa tank[5] and eating a vegetarian diet was no picnic for our young pre-novices. Fr. Mike was a credible prophet who was a true imitator of the Word-Deed (Jesus). To speak of the poor from ivory towers is much easier, but to live among the poor following their simple, albeit arduous lifestyle called for unmatched courage on one hand, and a certain degree of acceptance by and credibility among the poor on the other hand.[6]

What makes his option to live among the poor even more remarkable is the fact that Fr. Mike was presented with other more prominent (and lucrative) opportunities for his religious career. As a world-recognized theologian and religious scholar, he was regularly invited to religious conferences and theological conventions in Asia, Europe, and the United States. In 1978, he was offered a prestigious post as a professor at the Institut Catholique, Paris. Yet, he opted instead to enter the grueling heart of poverty in rural Sri Lanka, for it is there that he saw Christ manifested, and where he perceived his calling to witness Christ.

In light of the failed social revolution that had attempted to redress their situation by the poor youth of Sri Lanka in the form of the 1971 insurgency, the ethnic conflict raging in the northern regions of the country, and the emergent rumblings of a second youth insurgency in the 1980s in the southern, poverty-stricken areas, Fr. Mike had been questioning his role and the role of the church in ushering social justice. His poignant reflections on these concerns are clearly outlined in his second PhD thesis.

> As one who witnessed the bloody "insurrection" and revolt of the young people of Ceylon in 1971, I feel that the Church did very little

---

5. One of the local water reservoirs that is a part of the ancient cascade irrigation system, relied upon by the village people for their daily water needs.

6. Perera, personal communication, January 24, 2017.

at the time to help them. The token gift, however, of a few thousand rupees, handed by the leader of the Catholic Church in Ceylon, was misunderstood by the youth as a manner of perpetuating the injustices perpetrated, more in a social disorder than in a social order. Perhaps in the minds of these youth it looked like a peculiar way of closing the stable door after the horse had been stolen, and a way of setting aright by cure what was not done by prevention.[7]

In the aftermath of the brutal quelling of the first JVP uprising in 1973, Fr. Mike had penned the following words, which reflect his empathy for the spirit of the youth movement, including his concerns about their misguided methods:

> The youth of Sri Lanka set the example of a Passover. It may perhaps be that the matter of their struggle was absolutely correct but that the manner was wrong in the way they prepared for it and went about it "wantonly." . . . It is to the strength and courage of youth that Christ's beloved disciple addressed himself: "I am writing to you, young men, who have already overcome the Evil one: because you are strong and God's word has made its home in you" (1 John 2:13–14).[8]

Simultaneously, because of his firm conviction about the charge of Vatican II, Fr. Mike bemoaned the seeming inertia of the Church, especially the paucity of a dynamic engagement in redressing the historical injustices borne by the poor of Sri Lanka. His chagrin over this situation also stemmed from two other issues that perplexed him: what he perceived to be a resigned complacence in the church as an institution at that time to the plight of the poor, and the inadequacies in the training of seminarians to alleviate poverty.

> Fr. Mike believed that Christ, who is the irrevocable covenant of God with the oppressed of the earth, is the possible Christ of inter-religious dialogue. This Christ does not claim superiority over other religions but identifies himself with the masses of the oppressed and persecuted leading to dialogue at all levels. Thus an effective point of departure for dialogue would be the "liberation of the poor" from the human suffering caused by oppressive and unjust situations.
>
> —Silva, "Message," 18.

> If Vatican II suggested that seminarians "must be taught to look for Christ especially among the poor and the young" . . . it did not mean that this was a "pastime" only for those who are moving towards the priesthood. By a greater reason should this search be made sincere

---

7. Rodrigo, "Moral Passover," 117.
8. Ibid., 139.

and effective when those seminarians have finished their course and have become priests, bishops, and have instructed their lay-adults and their youth to see Christ in the poor and the young. True sympathy (sym-pathi) meaning to suffer with them, showing readiness to bear their burdens, and their willingness, correct their faults and re-live in a mere Christian manner their aspirations towards a just social order—youth have a right to all this.[9]

More specifically, he urged the church to prioritize poverty as a way to arrive at a submission to and oneness with Christ. He argued that when the church "gives priority of action to the poor in her pastoral action at every level, she is most herself, and so most Christ like."[10] He also made the case for the church serving as an example in this regard: "The Church is guided by Christ the great Liberator, but before she speaks to men about liberating themselves, her own example will be the best precept."[11]

Thus it appears that several forces culminated in Fr. Mike's decision to embark upon a submersion in poverty. Foremost among these was the profound transformation in his consciousness about the emblematic significance of the poor in Christian theology, together with a compelling yearning to serve the poor as his calling, forces which derived from his acute cognizance of the plight of the poor and the charge of Vatican II directives. Although these forces may have served as the catalyst for this move, no doubt the foundation of his quest for selfless immersion in ushering justice while witnessing to Christ's saving grace was long forged at an early age.

As Fr. Tissa Balasuriya mused in a dedication to Fr. Mike twelve days after his death,

> His interest in "Social Justice" was aroused by the movement and paper begun by Fr. Peter Pillai when he was at St. Peter's College. In the 1960s and 1970s, the Church and the Oblate Congregation took clear options in favor of the poor, of social justice,[12] of peace and dialogue with the other religions.[13]

---

9. Ibid., 117.
10. Ibid., 119–20.
11. Ibid., 121.
12. It is important to note that this commitment among the Oblate community of Sri Lanka (then known as Ceylon, still a part of the British Commonwealth) presaged the directives of Vatican II, which clearly articulated the call to service among the poor.
13. Balasuriya, "Fr. Michael Rodrigo OMI," 4.

This vision was further galvanized over the decade of the 1970s until he finally reached the decision to make a physical move to Buttala, a small but key town in the southwestern district of Moneragala, in a region referred to as Lower Uva (see map, p. 5). While the bulk of Sri Lanka's poor are still rural and primarily Buddhist, it was the historical significance of the area, its economic significance as the heart of poverty in Sri Lanka for several centuries, and its political significance as the center of the youth insurrection that rendered it a critical location for his work.

FORMING THE FAITH COMMUNITY AT SUBA SETH GEDERA[14]

In July 1980, Fr. Mike set out to Buttala with a Buddhist youth named Somadasa. Through their initial visits, Alukalavita village (approximately 4.6 kilometers from Buttala town center) was selected as the location to launch his immersion in redeeming the poor. Their first task was to learn about the people's aspirations in order to figure out how they would move forward on a collaboration with the villagers for their economic upliftment. Fr. Mike was able to secure a small plot of land in Alukalavita village to establish the residence that came to be known as Suba Seth Gedera (SSG).[15]

As evidence of his commitment to voluntary poverty, SSG consisted of a simple hut constructed of the same material as the dwellings in the

---

14. See also Fernando, *Harvest Dreams*.
15. Translated by Fr. Mike as "Good Wishes House."

village area, wattle and daub, and a roof thatched with the local *Iluk* grass. It had no electricity, indoor water, nor latrine facilities. Separate quarters were built on the premises for the two Salvatorian nuns who joined Fr. Mike approximately one year later. Given his penchant for precision and tendency to follow the Christian calendar, Fr. Mike had marked the two dates, the Feast Day of St. Anthony (June 13) as the date when SSG was established, and the Feast Day of St. Benedict (July 11) as the day when he was joined by the two nuns, Sr. Benedict Fernandopulle and Sr. Milburga Fernando. In addition, two recent university graduates, June Fernando and Priyanthi Perera, joined the group for the express purpose of undertaking a survey on the prevailing social and economic conditions of the area. Subsequently, a handful of locals supported the main activities of SSG: Dambegoda Jinadasa (who maintained the records), Sunethra Kulatunga, Rani Weerasuriya, and Sriyawathie Menike, who assisted the nuns in their respective activities.

The initiatives that Fr. Mike launched in Alukalavita village were devised in response to the abysmal lack of basic services, such as educational and health facilities, and the resultant low levels of literacy, low educational attainment and poor health care. Given the absence of qualified personnel to deliver these services, the two Salvatorian nuns proved indispensable to his mission.

> It is the imperious yet reassuring call of the Risen Christ hidden among the people, especially in the countryside. ("I'll go before you in to Galilee").
>
> —Rodrigo, "Hope of Liberation," 189.

Sr. Benedict, a trained nurse, and Sr. Milburga Fernando, an educationist, could well be thought of as representing Fr. Mike's right and left hand respectively, by carrying out the two main aspects of Fr. Mike's work in the village area (education and health). Each possessed a specialized skill and expertise invaluable for the mission of SSG, and shared Fr. Mike's deep devotion to the principle of caritas. They also grasped the significance of an outreach to the Buddhist poor. Unlike others he had initially broached the idea with, Sr. Benedict and Sr. Milburga were prepared to take up the challenge of a life with few amenities. Like Fr. Mike, they had adopted local garb, adjusted to the hardships of rural life, and interacted with the villagers in a manner that gave no hint of the class differences between them. Together with Fr. Mike, they were fully committed to the ultimate goal of restoring the dignity of the poor. Recollections by Sr. Milburga allow us a glimpse of the fascination and joy with which Fr. Mike embraced his life in Buttala, despite the hardships and challenges he encountered:

There, our lifestyle was very simple. Fr. Michael showed very little attachment to the usual amenities that he had been accustomed to. One exception was his library of books and notes that he had brought with him. How upset he was when moths and silver fish started attacking them! People and nature fascinated him. He spent much time listening to people. He was never too busy for them especially the children, who came along even to have their school books covered or to have their names written by him. At dawn and at dusk he listened to the cries of birds and animals, often imitating them. He would watch the sun rise and sun set, gazing on rocks, hills and far off mountains. Often he drew scenes and painted pictures and posters of them. His thoughts, feelings and experiences of these and other incidents emerged as poetry.[16]

Biographical note: Sr. Benedict Fernandopulle, SDS

A Salvatorian nun, Sr. Benedict is also a midwife and a skilled nurse trained in Italy and India. One of the founding members of Suba Seth Gedara, she was instrumental in leading the reproductive health program and the herbal medicine projects launched in the area. She also assumed responsibility for providing basic medical services to the community. Since Fr. Mike's untimely demise, she has continued working with the poor in other parts of Sri Lanka. Her efforts in this regard include economic empowerment of low income women in rural Kurunegala district and low-caste populations. She is currently engaged in these efforts in the Catholic Diocese of Kurunegala, Sri Lanka.

Biographical note: Sr. Milburga Fernando, SDS

After her theological studies in Rome, Sr. Milburga Fernando served as chaplain to the Catholic Students' Federation Sri Lanka from 1971 to 1974. Thereafter, she was attached to the Staff of *Sevaka Sevana*, Bandarawela, from 1974–1979. She was involved in a program of contextual theology envisioned by the Late Bishop Leo Nanayakkara, OSB, and actualized by Fr. Michael Rodrigo. She joined the team at Suba Seth Gedara in 1981, continuing her theological involvement in the Buddhist-Christian dialogue and conscientisation effort spearheaded by Fr. Michael Rodrigo. She presently works among the people in Kerawalapitiya-Hendala area, sharing their lives and issues from a theological perspective.

---

16. Fernando, "Fr. Michael Rodrigo OMI, as We Knew Him," 22.

TO BE THE POOR AND FOR THE POOR[17]: STRATEGIC ENTRY INTO THE HEART OF POVERTY

Located in the heart of Moneragala, the most poverty stricken district in the country, (see map, p. 54), the township of Buttala represented a strategic entry point for Fr. Mike's quest to witness Jesus to the poor and to witness the redemptive power of the poor to the nation, as well as the world at large. Given the sheer desolation and destitution across the area, it is no surprise that it was also a place where deep-seated disaffection had been slowly simmering among the youth. While their disillusionment is often attributed to the historical memory of conquest, exploitation, and oppression seared into the collective unconscious of the people of Uva, in reality, the long-standing social and economic marginality of the rural populace rendered the area rife with all the preconditions for social protest. It became the hotbed of the second JVP insurrection, which was just gathering force in the mid-1980s.

The surveys conducted by June Fernando and Priyanthi Fernando with Fr. Mike's guidance helped determine the gaps and needs of the population. At that time in the early 1980s, Alukalavita village was comprised of a population of approximately five hundred individuals, 20 percent of whom were under the age of five. The survey findings revealed the abysmal education and health situation in the area. Only a little over one-fifth (22 percent) of the population had completed their primary education, school drop-out rates were quite high (approximately one-fifth of school-goers opted out of school before grade five), and only a mere 7.5 percent had completed secondary school (the GCE or Ordinary Level Exam in the British system). Less than one percent (.75) had an education beyond grade eight. Waguruwela Maha Vidyalaya (WMV), the main school serving the larger area, catered to approximately eight hundred and fifty students from grade one to eleven, taught

> His understanding of Buddhism and identification with village life, its culture and its poverty, his grasp of the problems confronting the peasants, his espousal of justice and intervention whether on behalf of the poor villagers or the workers of the multinational close by at Pelwatte, more than established his bona fides and endeared him to the people.
>
> —*Christian Workers Fellowship.*

---

17. The notion of being one with the poor (through a voluntary embrace of poverty), and to work for the poor is also one articulated by Fr. Aloy Pieris (see "To Be Poor"), in honoring God's covenant with the poor, and in emulating God's divine struggle for the poor.

by about thirty five teachers (with a teacher/student ratio of 1:25), much higher than the more prestigious school adjacent to Buttala town, Dutugemunu Central College. The attrition rates at WMV were quite high due to the inability of many families to keep children in school during peaks in the cultivation cycle, and early withdrawal from school (as youth had no choice but to support the agricultural activities of their family through their full-time labor contributions).

Most villagers qualified for the food stamp scheme, and drought aid, but did not receive the latter regularly due to political interference.[18] Many worked as day laborers (some as young as fifteen, both male and female alike) on the sugar cane fields of the adjoining Pelwatte Sugar Corporation (PSC), where they worked long hours under arduous conditions.[19] Accustomed to rice farming for generations, most continued to plant small plots of rice, while many had forfeited their rice land due to their inability to repay debts to local moneylenders. Indebtedness was high in the area, due mainly to loans taken in advance under usurious terms for the purchase of agricultural inputs, given that financial assets and savings were difficult to shore up. Harvests lost due to the recurrent droughts, perennial water shortages, and the virtual absence of an irrigation infrastructure in the area compounded the problem. Ironically, three hundred years prior to this, the entire area was a thriving rice economy reliant on the intricate irrigation network put in place by the Sinhala royalty. The destruction of that irrigation infrastructure by British colonial authorities attempting to quell the peasant uprising of 1818 is recognized as the main reason for the erosion of subsistence security of the farming population of Uva, further clarified below.

BRIDGING THE URBAN-RURAL DIVIDE

The significance of Fr. Mike's work among the poor of rural Lanka must also be understood in terms of the age-long, urban-rural divide in the country. As in most developing nations, the urban center(s) dominated the national landscape not only as the locus of power, but also in terms of development. The rural periphery on the other hand has languished at the

---

18. A common practice in distant locations was to deny the social protection payments to individuals who had not voted for the politically powerful in the area.

19. As the author's research on PSC has documented, and typical of work on sugar plantations around the world, their working conditions were grueling at best. See, for example, Gunewardena, "Bitter Cane."

physical, social, economic, and cultural margins of the nation. The glaring lack of physical infrastructure (traversable roads and transportation) not only within the rural periphery, but also between urban and rural areas that prevailed in the 1980s in Sri Lanka meant that those residing in the towns surrounding the capital city travelled out infrequently, and vice versa. As a result, urbanites operated on the basis of superficial impressions and misconceptions about the real life conditions of the masses of farming communities. This continues to be the case even today, and even among those whose careers are built on matters pertaining to the rural, i.e., policymakers, high-level government officials,[20] academics, and researchers. This author was surprised to learn that she was only one of two anthropologists[21] to have undertaken ethnographic research in situ[22] in Moneragala district in decades.

The rural-urban divide was also manifested in stark gaps in the quality of life indicators between the two areas. Glaring disparities along key measures such as literacy and education outcomes, maternal and child nutrition and health, and poverty attested to that long prevailing divide. Moreover, a latent class snobbery that hints of neo-colonial influences has long characterized the rural population as backward *(pitisara)*, under-developed *(nodiyunu)* and uneducated *(noogath)*. Cognizant of such caricatures of representation, the rural poor seemed to have internalized a sense of inferiority. Although a few avenues to social mobility were open to them through semi-skilled, small business ventures and and even the rare chance to gain entrance to university, for most rural people, such opportunities were foreclosed simply by virtue of the under-resourced and under-staffed education facilities in the rural periphery. The stigma attached to the rural thus has contributed to the sting of marginality experienced by rural populations. Youth who somehow overcame these odds and managed to gain entrance to and complete their university education were keen to overturn

---

20. Policymakers and high-level government officials relied on the information provided by provincial and district authorities, most of whom were equally unlikely to have intimate knowledge of the interior, given the poor conditions and difficult environment. This was confirmed by this author's discussions with key government representatives during her tenure as the Social Sector Coordinator for the World Bank operations in Sri Lanka.

21. The other being a US-based anthropologist, Michael D. Woost, PhD (Hartwick College), who studied the economy of Okkampitiya, a gem mining area a few kilometers from Alukalavita village.

22. Which entailed long-term residence within a village, in order to undertake research based on the methodology of participant observation.

their secondary status in the society—the precursor to the JVP youth insurgency. As an astute observer of human nature, Fr. Mike would have realized that it was not merely the grueling aspects of their concrete life conditions that drove youth in the area to join the JVP, but also their consciousness of their *symbolic* marginality in the social and political landscape of the nation.

Ironically, there was a national tendency to romanticize the rural, with gross over-generalizations of the rural as an idyllic setting, imbued with serenity and harmony, as depicted in many vernacular songs, poetry, and novels that attempted to capture folk life in Sri Lanka. Yet, most middle-class and elite individuals preferred the amenities and comforts of urban life. Apart from their occasional forays beyond the urbanized areas, rural Sri Lanka remained distant and cut-off from the rest of the country. As a result, the rural periphery was for the most part understood through gross generalizations or glossy misrepresentations. These depictions obscured the often class and caste stratified fabric of rural life, especially with the influx of modernization, which was often accompanied by corruption and greed. The exploitation of the poor not only by a new trading class, but also by corporate interests and powerful individuals who had accumulated wealth through nefarious means was the insidious underbelly of rural life.

These were the realities Fr. Mike grappled with as he encountered rural life during his teaching years at Ampitiya and Sevaka Sevana seminaries, and in his work at SSG. He was deeply troubled by the egregious injustices and flagrant violations of basic human rights that were an inherent part of the lives of rural people. The very indignity of poverty alone evoked in him a near-compulsion to redress the wrongs endured by the poor.

> **The 1818 Uva-Vellassa Uprising**
>
> Historical records denote an uprising that took place in 1818 by the farming communities of Uva against the British colonial government. After a series of skirmishes, the British managed to suppress the uprising by resorting to the excessive tactics of killing the entire able-bodied male population of the Uva region above the age of 18 years, destroying homes and the small irrigation systems known as "tanks" across the entire region, poisoning water wells, killing all cattle and other domesticated animals, and burning all cultivated fields in the area. This scorched-earth policy resulted in the complete devastation of the lives and livelihood security of the region.

> If development is truly de-envelopment, the removing of the envelope of bonds, then true development and liberation coincide

in the release of the broken, and in transformation, not in mere reform for the oppressive and exploitative economic, social, political, cultural structures in to a new society. Then respect for human dignity becomes the creating of a society based on people's needs. If we are committed to them, involved with them and among them, rather than working for them, the very process of decision making with them will become a transforming process. We—the Jesus community—will not be mere catalysis, for in the process of a mutual presence, the people and we will be "doing the truth in love" and that transforms us both, when people become the architects of their own destiny.[23]

A vision of the poor as authors of their future, as 'architects of their own destiny' seems to have spurred on Fr. Mike's quest for social justice. As the next section discusses, it is fair to say that the sheer denial of human rights that contravened the shaping of one's destiny would have pierced his heart.

MORAL INDIGNATION OF THE HISTORICAL INJUSTICES ENDURED BY THE PEOPLE OF BUTTALA

Prior to the period of British colonial rule, the Uva-Vellassa area of southeastern Sri Lanka (then Ceylon) was a thriving rice farming economy, considered the granary of the kingdom. So named for the thousand small irrigation works (*Vel Laksa*[24]) that fed the rice paddies, it was primarily a subsistence oriented economy, although a proportion of their harvest was expected to be delivered to the governing royalty, a customary practice in many such systems around the world. Despite the assurance of water through the irrigation infrastructure (a series of cascading reservoirs locally referred to as "tanks"), the eco-climatic conditions of the Dry Zone entails chronic subsistence insecurity. Perhaps precisely because of the latter, kin and social ties were highly valued as a source of "social security," often referred to in contemporary parlance as a "safety net." Given this situation of uncertainty, any external threat to their subsistence security is thus likely to have prompted resistance and protest, as argued by the anthropologist James C. Scott, in his book, *The Moral Economy of the Peasant* (1976). Scott argued that, in fact, outright and full scale rebellions have

---

23. Rodrigo, "Hope of Liberation," 193.

24. Literal translation is a thousand reservoirs from Sinhala. *Vel* means reservoirs; *Laksa* means thousand.

occurred in the case of excessive imposition of taxes or corvée labor, as in Vietnam and Myanmar (then referred to as Burma), which detracted from the subsistence cushion of peasant populations. These practices were also common during the period of British colonization in Sri Lanka (then known as Ceylon), when usurious taxation schemes and labor obligations were imposed on the farming communities of the country, not only as a means of financing the colonial administration, but also admittedly to prompt the native population to submit to the authority of the British.

As historical records indicate, when these proudly self-reliant farming communities refused to do so, a campaign to pressure the population through even more coercive means was launched by the colonial administration. Indignant populations of the Uva area responded by staging an uprising, the first major rebellion against British rule.[25] The response was a General Order issued in 1818 by the main colonial representative in power over the island, Governor Brownrigg with instructions for a ruthless scorched-earth campaign intended to stem the rebellion. British troops were ordered to kill every man, woman, and child, burn all dwellings and crops, including fruit trees and rice paddies. The embankments of the irrigation reservoir system, including the main canals and artery channels, were destroyed. Some accounts report the poisoning of wells and the slaughter of cattle. The resulting devastation of their subsistence infrastructure forced the people of Uva-Vellassa to scatter to remote parts of the island. Some retreated further into the jungle and reverted to slash-and-burn cultivation *(hen or chena* farming), effectively reversing the trajectory of their economic development and subjecting them to perennial livelihood insecurity as well as social marginality.

In keeping with Scott's argument, we may surmise that the destruction of their subsistence base together with the imposition of colonial strictures that severely undermined their subsistence security was perceived as a violation of their "moral economy" by the people of lower Uva. Fr. Mike fully grasped the significance of this event as indeed a moral violation, and often recalled how the memory of the 1818 rebellion lingered in the collective consciousness of the people of Uva. Since they had never fully recovered from the devastation of that period, and given that subsequent national governments since independence (1948) had focused much of its development efforts in the urban center, the populations of Uva harbored a strong sense of being overlooked and marginalized. Indeed, the absence of

---

25. See Obeyesekere, "Colonial Rape."

a functional infrastructure well into the 1970s and 1980s (and even decades thereafter), including transportation, communication, and basic services (e.g., health and education facilities) in lower Uva bore witness to this reality. As Fr. Claude Perera notes,

> He wanted to recompense somehow for the acts of the colonizers, not merely through monetary means, but also to redeem their dignity. Lower Uva was thus critical for his vision of embracing the poor and voluntary poverty.[26]

To further complicate this situation, in the early 1980s a decision was made to introduce commercial scale sugar cane cultivation in the area, as part of a strategy for employment creation and poverty alleviation, through the neoliberal bent of the "Open Economy" policies advocated by the United National Party (UNP) that came into power in 1972. Regrettably, the introduction of large scale sugar production set off yet another cycle of poverty and disempowerment. Many in the Buttala area were cajoled off their land for the establishment of a commercial sugar plantation, the Pelwatte Sugar Corporation (PSC), while others were coaxed to shift from subsistence crops to sugar cane, with the promise of high incomes. Repetitive droughts and wild-elephant damage to crops, however, meant that such returns could hardly be realized. The end result being that a bulk of the population was slowly converted to working as dependent wage-laborers on PSC (a joint venture between the Sri Lanka government and the industrial sugar giant, Booker-Tate International). They were robbed of the sense of autonomy they had been accustomed to from time immemorial, as an independent and industrious farming population.

Upon his entry into the area, Fr. Mike was incensed by what he witnessed. Given his assiduous scholarly nature, he started researching and documenting the exploitative practices in the area, and how the poor were preyed upon by power-hungry politicians, avaricious money lenders, and exploitative corporations alike. He raised awareness of these issues through his lectures in Sri Lanka and around the world, and reported his findings in a stream of letters to various government authorities. He realized that the rural poor were subjected not only to a historical injustice (i.e., during the colonial era), but also to ongoing atrocities. In Fr. Claude Perera's view, "Fr. Mike felt that God's covenant with the poor had been violated

---

26. Perera, personal communication, July 2016.

by their ongoing oppression, and he was keen to emulate the spirit of Poor Jesus."[27] In order to redress these wrongs, Fr. Mike felt that it was necessary to endure the trials faced by the poor. "We must also suffer the pain of our neglect and abandoning of the peasants for too long."[28]

It was thus for the twin goals of correcting the centuries-old economic and social disempowerment of the people of Vellassa, and his yearning to witness Christ to the poor as a process of spiritual and economic liberation for them, that Fr. Mike launched the work at SSG.

> Suba Seth Gedera, although eventually possessing a classroom and health room as well as living quarters, was built largely of local materials and had no electricity or piped water.
>
> —Harris, "Double Belonging," 82.

PRACTICING SELFLESSNESS

In establishing SSG, Fr. Mike practiced renunciation to the extreme. As noted above, he forsook all comfort, donned the simplest of garments worn by the locals and managed with no creature comforts nor amenities. He slept on a mat woven of coconut palm, wore local garb (cassock replaced with a sarong and tunic), and simple slippers.[29] On one occasion when one of the nuns had voiced her concern over the constant back pain that Fr. Mike suffered due to the hard wooden surface he slept on, he retorted that since the villagers customarily slept on equally hard surfaces, he would not indulge in any comforts either. Whenever he had to travel to Colombo, he was known to walk the nearly three miles to the main bus stand in Buttala town, and wait patiently along with locals who had no other means of transportation for the rickety bus that

> Fr. Mike lived Christianity. He was not just another Christian but another Christ. He was willing to make meaningful sacrifices and live a life of holiness; total, complete and personal assimilation of gospel values as a unique mode of life on behalf of the suffering masses in Buttala. He was committed to carrying the cross of Christ in a God-forsaken corner in Sri Lanka. The cross represents a challenge to the total person. It asks for a total involvement on behalf of suffering humanity.
>
> —Meemana, Untitled account, para. 15.

---

27. Ibid.
28. Rodrigo, "Notes."
29. Attested to by the author, who visited SSG on several occasions in 1987 while she was conducting her own PhD research in the nearby Pelwatte Sugar Corporation, and by Elisabeth Harris, British religious studies scholar who spent several years studying interfaith dialogue in Sri Lanka and also visited SSG in 1985–86.

would carry them on the twelve-hour journey under cramped and crowded conditions.

These acts of self-sacrifice illustrated on one hand his deep conviction that Christianity embodied the virtue of selflessness, but also his affinity with the poor. He wanted to erase as far as possible any distinctions between himself and the poor in terms of social and economic status, religious affiliation, class, language, etc. The virtue of self-sacrifice he practiced is also inextricably linked with his striving for detachment, a key tenet in Buddhism as well as Christianity. As Harris has clarified this tendency in Christin mystical tradition, "detachment from material concerns has been considered essential if there is to be a movement toward God."[30]

ACTIVIST COMPASSION

A profound compassion for the poor was at the heart of Fr. Mike's decision to leave the comfortable trappings of the church and search for ways to truly serve the poor. His understanding of compassion was through Christ's teachings as well as Buddhist notions of *karuna* and *metta*, as expounded in his doctoral theses. Most importantly, Fr. Mike's life and work, his journey for justice for the poor embodies much more than the sentiment or subjective understanding of compassion. He infused it with action in the way Harris has clarified,

> Engaged Buddhism is Buddhism that takes activist compassionate action into the heart of politics, conflict mediation and social action.[31]

At the heart of his compassion, moreover, was a profound upwelling of empathy and a remarkable altruism[32] that emanated from a genuine concern for the poor. It was in the classic sense of altruism that prompts a person to take actions that may put themselves at risk or entail extreme self-sacrifice. As Sr. Benedict, whom this author would herald as Fr. Mike's right hand, noted in a personal communication with the author, "he suffered *with* the poor." He had entered their suffering in a way that he, himself experienced the range of anguish, despair, desolation, and abandonment

---

30. Harris, *Buddhism*, 74.

31. Ibid., 78.

32. This type of altruism is considered rare empirical frequency, given the norm of self-interest that predominates human behavior. See Monroe, *Heart of Altruism*.

they faced. This visceral suffering deepened his convictions to usher correctives to the historical injustices the people of Buttala had endured. In all his interactions with the poor, not only did he exemplify compassion, but

> The poor suffer. We must wipe the tears of suffering from their eyes. If we don't, then someday, God will have his way. *Ochlos* is mentioned very significantly in *Apocalypse*: *"After this I saw a great crowd Ochlos whom no man could number"* (Revelation 7:9ff).
>
> Just now Uva offers this situation. We too have been called upon to help people, to realise their hidden power and to wipe away the tears from their eyes: the eyes of the Ochlos.
>
> —Rodrigo (excerpts from unpublished notes, Beginnings of Suba Seth Gedera).

also a perceptive tolerance. Even in his corrective efforts with youth or in mediating a situation, he was known to have used humor, adhering vocally to the caution in Prov 15:1: "A soft answer turns away wrath."

DIALOGUE AS THE ROUTE TO PARTICIPATORY DEVELOPMENT

Suba Seth Gedera epitomized Fr. Mike's dialogue in action formulation, which served as a vehicle to embark upon his immersion among the poor. The village dialogue process that Fr. Mike had developed was not conceptualized as a top-down process of leading the poor to justice. More powerfully, it was envisioned as a *participatory* process undertaken through a dialogue that was designed to honor the wishes, priorities, experience, native knowledge, and traditions of the local population. This approach was clarified by Fr. Mike in a paper he presented at the Buddhist-Christian Conference in Berkeley, California, in August 1987, a mere three months prior to his passing.

> Our Village Dialogue effort is but a promising preamble to solidarity in this emerging world-wide community: the Poor coming into their own as masters and subjects of their destiny. Such a dialogue will keep Buddhism and Christianity ever vigilant. Village or world social relationships are wrecked when gathered around counter-values of wealth, money, worldliness, sin. They are fostered and deepened when gathered round the pole of values like poverty, detachment, no-avarice, authority as service, fellowship and brotherhood/sisterhood of humans.[33]

33. Rodrigo, "Example Village Dialogue", 7, para. 3.

As a scholar not only of theology, but also of national and local development, social justice, and human rights, Fr. Mike was well versed in the tenets of participatory development (PD) that emerged in the 1970s as a vehement counter to the "top-down" approaches to development that had prevailed until then. Fr. Mike was inherently an advocate of the foundational stance in PD that local populations should be actively engaged in the development process in shaping their self-empowerment, thus influencing the direction of their development, assuming ownership and control of the type of development. Thus, the concept of village dialogue that Fr. Mike initiated was meant to give voice to the poor, to hear and learn about their views, priorities, and needs, and to register the value of their perspectives. In the first year of his move to Buttala, therefore, Fr. Mike emphasized the importance of "moving with the people," of observing and participating in their quotidian world.

An essential part of his village dialogue concept was to reside among the poor, in as far as possible under the same grueling conditions as they did, in an effort to erase (or at least minimize) the differences (in education, knowledge, language, social background) between the faith community he represented and the poor in Buttala. A concerted attention to these issues paved the way for establishing trust and mutual understanding—noteworthy indeed, given the context of local suspicions about the possible sinister motives behind a Catholic priest's interest in a Buddhist village area (i.e., conversion). Once the fear that he would undertake conversions had been dispelled, the ongoing dialogue deepened into a consultative process where the villagers identified their main concerns: the lack of land, water shortages and drought conditions, livelihood insecurity, seasonal hunger, undernutrition, the lack of health facilities, and low educational outcomes.

Fr. Mike was a firm believer in the power of the poor to harness their energies in a self-reliant form of development. While he exemplified tremendous compassion for them, he also saw them as capable of determining the direction of their lives and in undertaking appropriate decisions that would improve their lot. In this manner, he understood that a genuine dialogue entailed a collaborative identification of the most pressing challenges faced by the poor. He relied on the process of conscientization to guide them to analyze the critical issues they faced, with the ensuing dialogue as a vital, engaged, solution-seeking exchange.

From the start, SSG doors were open to the village, and soon a trickle of youth, village elders, and women became regular visitors who asked questions, made requests, and often challenged and debated issues with Fr. Mike until an understanding of his quest emerged. As a result of this process, several activities to improve the lives of the surrounding community were launched: the herbarium to promote indigenous sources of healing, a preschool (Montessori), English classes for the youth, a library, distribution of coconut seedlings, toilets for individual village homes (with donor funding Fr. Mike had secured) and a host of other much needed programs.

The collaborative nature of all these endeavors is confirmed by the formation of a cooperative entity in the village area called "Minis Samagi Havula," literally translated as "People's Joint Venture." When the idea of opening a preschool in the village was first broached by this group in 1985, Fr. Mike had emphatically supported it, given his belief in the power of education: "Education should be the vehicle to teach humanness and human values. The school provides the ambit to share and experience these values."[34]

> In 1980, Fr. Mike began his mission in the village of Buttala, to bring the Word of God among the majority Buddhist population. There, he lived in a small mud hut. His focus on enculturation, interreligious dialogue and integration did not please the Church hierarchy. He was with the people and helped them to understand how they risked being exploited by the world of politics and business. In what many called his "ashram", he set in act a genuine freedom movement. Fr. Mike incorporated the principles of the liberation in Buddhism, and brought Christianity and a new awareness among people.
>
> —Fernando, "Fr. Mike, Prophet and Martyr," para. 3.

LIVING AMONG THE POOR, PRESENTING JESUS TO THE POOR

It was his conviction that in order to engage with the Buddhist poor in spiritual praxis, he needed to live among them, and live like them. He believed that this was also Christ's call for humanity, to relinquish all comforts. In keeping with this conviction, he chose a residence that was like most dwelling structures of the poorest of the poor in the heartland of rural poverty in Sri Lanka—as noted above, constructed of mud, sticks, and clay. Over time, some of the dwelling area at SSG got a cement floor, while others remained coated in the clay and cow dung typical of village homes across Asia. Portions of the main house got a tin roof as the years proved hard for the Iluk grass thatch to shelter the home from heavy seasonal rains. He settled on the name "Suba Seth Gedera," translated best as "Good Wishes House" to

---

34. Fernando, "Fr. Michael Rodrigo OMI, as We Knew Him," 24.

register his intentions. It was a place of faith practice, bereft of the typical markings of a church, purposefully left that way in order to signify it as an open home for Buddhist and Christian alike, and to foreclose the possibility of being interpreted as solely a place of worship for Christians alone.

As noted above, approximately a year after he set out to launch SSG, two Salvatorian nuns joined Fr. Mike—Sr. Benedict Fernandopulle, SDS, with a diploma in nursing (gynecology), and Sr. Milburga Fernando, SDS, who held a diploma in theology (Rome) and had six years of experience teaching theology to high school students and the seminarians in the Uva Diocese. Sr. Milburga, whom this author would classify as Fr. Mike's left hand, assumed responsibility together with Fr. Mike to conduct the educational programs. Village children were given English lessons, tutored to pass their exams, and assisted with their homework. Sr. Benedict who would indeed be deemed his right hand, served the community through a health outreach program. She provided reproductive health services to the women, performed midwifery services, trained a group of young village girls as barefoot nurses, and provided essential prenatal and postnatal care and guidance to the entire village area. In a district served by one small, inadequately equipped rural hospital, these services proved to be invaluable for the quality of life and wellbeing among the poor masses. A monthly clinic day was attended by people from seventeen nearby villages, an herbarium was planted on the premises of SSG and herbal gardens were introduced to the four temples in the area, with young girls trained to plant and nurture them, and instructed on the benefits of each by Sr. Benedict. SSG thus became a center for teaching and healing.

Other initiatives for social wellbeing and economic empowerment launched by Fr. Mike included an organic fertilizer program with village youth trained in its production, introduction of coconut seedlings (now fully fruit bearing), a latrine construction program for every household (partially funded through donor contributions Fr. Mike had secured), a Montessori school, exam preparation tuition for youth sitting for the Ordinary-Level and Advanced-Level exams (equivalent of grade 10 and 12 respectively in the U.S. educational system), a literacy and numeracy program for the school drop-outs, English classes for job aspirants, a newspaper reading program, a media library that included slides and other audio-visual material on important topics from world news to environmental protection, and many others. A commemorative article that appeared in the Sri Lankan newspaper, *Ceylon Today*, on the anniversary of Fr. Mike's death in 2014, refers to how he was "inspired by the fervor of service to the people" and "wanted to reach out to all the people" to improve their "human welfare and wellbeing." Indeed, the reinvigoration of the Buttala area that transpired through Fr. Mike's presence and efforts is remembered with affection and reverence:

As Robert Traer, executive director of the International Association for Religious Freedom from 1990 to 2000 writes,

> Moreover, in a Sri Lankan village Buddhists and Roman Catholics have found a common cause in human rights. In 1981, before a thousand people gathered to celebrate the triple light festival of Vesak, recalling the birth, enlightenment and the *mahaparinibbana* of the Buddha, a Christian speaker[35] suggested: "if we violate human rights for food, clothing, shelter, justice, then we violate the first precept: *pranatipata vera mani sikkha*."[36] ... The Venerable Kotaneluwe Upatissa of the ancient Happoruwa temple, who was present for the festival at Suba Seth Gedara on this occasion, replied: "Let me say that this Catholic priest expounded dhamma well. Similarly, when Buddhists and Christians joined together to seek help for farmers who had lost their harvest due to severe drought, the Venerable Alutwela Piyananda—although pressured by local officials not to participate in the petition—affirmed instead his unity with the Christians in their common cause: "For whom did Jesus live and die? for man. For whom did the Buddha work? for man, for men and women. Now let us get together and work for human rights."[37]

> He also maintained a running dialogue with Buddhist monks in the area. At the start of his mission in Buttala, the villagers and Buddhist monks in the area were skeptical about his motives and those of his co-workers. In fact one monk is said to have remarked that it would not be long before he started pouring the waters of baptism on unsuspecting villagers. The sincerity of his motives and his carefully designed programme of work in the village finally convinced these monks, that in him they had found a loyal and sincere partner in pursuing the goal of moral regeneration and joint social validation of religion.
>
> —Wijeyeratne, "Harvest Dream," para. 5.

conference called "Buddhism and Christianity: Toward the Human Future," in Berkeley, California.

36. This first precept entailed abstaining from taking life, in whatever form, animal or human, harking back to and related to the notion of ahimsa, discussed earlier (see chapter 1).

37. Traer, "Buddhist Affirmations," 17.

ROOTEDNESS IN CHRISTIAN SPIRITUALITY, SERVING THE POOR AND ENGAGING BUDDHIST BELIEVERS

From all available accounts, including Fr. Mike's writing and conference presentations, it is clear that he remained firmly rooted in Christianity while working on behalf of and with the Buddhist poor. Scholarly analysis of this type of process focuses on two related aspects of a life of service: religious "belonging" and identity. The central question in this regard is whether it is possible to claim multiple religious belonging, and whether doing so represents a quandary for Christian spiritual identity and practice. According to Harris, although key religious figures such as Fr. Mike chose a life of service among the Buddhist poor, it may not be equated with multiple religious belonging. This is, in fact, confirmed by what we know from Fr. Mike's exemplary life—not only did he remain a Christian, but his work among the Buddhist poor deepened his Christianity in an extraordinary manner. As Fredericks clarifies,

> Buddhist communities welcomed them and provided a supportive environment in which they practiced their Christian spirituality. Buddhism itself became a way for these Christians to think about their own faith and live it out in new ways.[38]

Indeed, the reflections above attest to the open-minded manner in which Fr. Mike sought to engage the Buddhist sangha and lay community, eager to learn from them and to continue honing his understanding of the universal parallels between the two faiths. As the head monk of Buttala noted (see box below, on page 79), Fr. Mike participated regularly in the Buddhist prayer and rituals of the area, while engaging in theological discussions with the sangha. Scholars such as Peter Phan (2003) who have embarked on lengthy analysis of multiple religious belonging center their arguments on the possibility of accommodating or adopting the beliefs and practices of other religions. Phan argues, for example that,

> In Asian countries such as China, Japan, Korea, Vietnam, India, Nepal and Sri Lanka, multiple religious belonging is a rule rather than an exception, at least on the popular level.[39]

He proceeds to clarify, however, that there are instances in which the degree of closed-ness (for lack of a better word) or exclusivity is dependent

---

38. Fredericks, "*Many Mansions?*: Multiple Religious Belonging," 169–70.
39. Phan, "Multiple Belonging," 498.

on the extent to which it may have been denigrated by another faith. Alluding to the case of Buddhism in Sri Lanka, he argues,

> Furthermore, at times, a religion which is not by nature exclusive only becomes so as a reaction to the claims of superiority made by Christianity, as it happened to Buddhism in Sri Lanka in the 19th century, and then the relationship between the two religions becomes that of competition rather than peaceful co-existence.[40]

The initial reaction from the area's Buddhist monk was to warn his Buddhist faithful that Michael was a Catholic missionary who would entice the unsuspecting villages, by foreign donations. "He would pour water over your heads and convert you to Christianity" said the monk. But Mike's mission methods were nowhere close what the monk had suspected. Mike first became a close friend and confidante of the monk. Then they worked together to improve neglected conditions of education and sanitation in the village.

One day, the monk sent for Mike and informed him that he had to be away from the temple on some important business and that he was in search of someone to deliver the usual weekly instruction on Saturday to his faithful. Mike wanted the monk to name his substitute, promising to see to it that the substitute monk would be brought to the temple in time. The monk smiled and to Mike's surprise said, "Well, you are the one best suited to undertake that task." Mike did undertake the onerous task. His presentation on the values of the religions was so well received that from then onwards, every first Saturday, it was Mike who instructed the Buddhist faithful. They remained good Buddhists, but with great respect for the Christianity that Mike testified by his life.

—OMI Mission, "Michael Rodrigo—Dialogue as Mission," para. 4.

While this tendency is apparent in the current violent stand-off between Islam and Christianity, in the case of Sri Lanka, historical records bear ample evidence of a virulent vilification of Buddhism by church authorities during the colonial era. For Fr. Mike, being acutely conscious of this divisive and damaging trend in national history, the fundamental question seems not to have been about religious identity as much as a pressing concern to bridge the two faith traditions through an empathetic understanding and a vocal acknowledgement of the virtues of Buddhism.

All throughout, nonetheless, Fr. Mike remained firmly grounded in his faith and his belief in the divinity of Christ. His mission at Suba Seth Gedera was not grounded in a proselytizing vision, nor one that rested on undertaking conversions. Therein lay the effectiveness of his outreach to the Buddhist poor in Buttala. He was not interested in claiming the kind

---

40. Ibid., 499.

of multiple religious belonging where he would practice Buddhist rituals, nor expect Buddhists to follow Christian rituals. He was convinced that there was a deeper and more fundamental truth—the adherence to sound moral practices, and "elements of truth and grace"[41] common to most religious traditions.[42] In other words, he found Buddhism to be a source of inspiration and spiritual enrichment that did not require an embrace of "belonging" nor a dual identity, as in Cornille's scheme. Similarly, it would be difficult to conclude as per Phan, that Fr. Mike chose to "follow" some of the doctrinal teachings and religious practices of Buddhism, an option for those who choose multiple religious belonging, given his single-minded devotion to Christ.

Although he participated in the annual cycle of ritual worship observed by the Buddhist communities of Buttala, he did so to register respect, tolerance, and acceptance of the basic tenets of Buddhism. Neither did Fr. Mike attempt to "go over"[43] to Buddhism in an effort to deepen his Christian identity. From all verifiable accounts, Fr. Mike remained a deeply resolute and devoted Christian. True to Phan's argument, Fr. Mike's quest in developing the "Buddhist-Christian Dialogue" and in engaging the Buddhist poor of Lanka did not originate from any form of uncertainty about his Christian identity.[44] It was certainly not a crisis in faith, nor based on even an iota of doubt "about the unique and universal role of Christ as the savior"[45] that led him to this engagement. Instead, as Phan argues, referring to Fr. Mike in particular and to other leading religious figures such as Fr. Aloysius Pieris of Sri Lanka,

> their religious quest was deeply rooted in their Christian faith, and indeed, it was their Christian conviction that revelation and salvation, brought about by Jesus, is somehow present in other religious traditions, that set them in their journey.[46]

Disenchantment with the church was, however, something that Fr. Mike struggled with, especially in terms of what he saw as the lack of a

---

41. Ibid., 504.
42. As detailed in one of Fr. Mike's doctoral theses.
43. Phan, "Multiple Belonging," 506.
44. Ibid., 508.
45. Ibid., 509.
46. Ibid., 509. It is important to note that although Phan ends this statement with the phrase "of multiple religious belonging," the author refrains purposefully from including it, given her conviction that Fr. Mike was not interested in claiming a multiple religious affinity.

sufficient outreach to the poor. In like manner, the church at the time was sometimes critical of Fr. Mike's particular ideas and approaches. As such, it took much soul searching and immense courage for Fr. Mike to step beyond the boundaries of his priestly mission as the church saw it, to embark on establishing a space of love and interfaith meeting of hearts and minds. Considered a pioneer in retrospect, Fr. Mike's work at SSG, and his engagement with the Buddhist communities is considered an exemplary, if not a unique and inspirational example of interfaith dialogue by scholars undertaking any analysis of interfaith ministry.

RIGHTEOUS ANGER, PACIFIST STRATEGIES, AND THE LOVE COMMANDMENT

As much as Fr. Mike abhorred violence, especially violence deployed against the vulnerable and as a means to achieving power, and even though he advocated for and encouraged nonviolent approaches to addressing the social injustices of the day, he railed against the wrongs of the world. It was a righteous anger that gripped him, and that drove his passion for redress. Examples of righteous anger in the Bible include David's exclamation, "God, I wish you would kill the wicked!" (Ps 139:19) and Nehemiah's fulmination against the exploitation of the poor by wealthy Israelites, "Then I was very angry when I had heard . . . these words" (Neh 5:6). We are even offered a glimpse of Jesus' righteous anger upon encountering the conduct of commercial activities that sullied the sanctity of the temple (Matt 21:12–13; Luke 19:45–48). In like manner, Fr. Mike was no doubt outraged by the sheer magnitude and boldness of the exploitation the poor in Buttala had been subjected to for decades, if not centuries.

As a virtuous man, however, and one mindful of modeling right conduct from a Christian and Buddhist perspective, he was careful about how he managed and expressed that righteous anger. In a poem penned on June 30, 1987, his sixtieth birthday, and a mere four months before his untimely demise, he acknowledges the righteous anger that had been welling up in him.[47] Yet, he channeled his anger toward redemptive action-strategies designed to uplift the poor in a self-reliant, resilient, and sustainable manner—because he was firmly grounded in a pacifist spirit. Nonetheless, all throughout, he resorted to expressing his concerns and observations through forthright and critical letters to government authorities, virtually

---

47. Poem entitled "For a Faith Vision at Sixty," full text at the end of the chapter.

"raising hell" by his meticulous documentation of each instance and act of exploitation experienced by the poor. The sense of enragement Fr. Mike experienced fueled his drive to somehow stem the tide of the historical and contemporary forms of oppression endured by the poor. His sharp wit became a tool in exposing the duplicity of powerful forces. Although he would have been aware of the extent to which he was endangering his own life by speaking out boldly against the powers that be, it was a risk he was prepared to take. The impulse of self-sacrifice that he seemed to have internalized so deeply propelled him forward in taking on the task of restoring the rights of the poor, even at the jeopardy to his life.

FOR A FAITH VISION AT SIXTY

Sisters, I am growing old,
I've no silver, I've no gold
But we've come a very long way
Through the fields of new-mown hay
The poor will always all recall us
As a group that loves them true
Yes, my sisters, we and they are one
Till the sands of life are run.

Years have fled, let us recall,
Greet His blessings one and all
Still the savior tells his lowly bride:
"You are ever fair, my pride"
Holds them in his heart aglow
Silver sheen or golden glow
Yes, dear Sisters, you must know
He will never let us go.

Sixty years upon this earth
Since my mother gave me birth
Sixty years of heavy burden
For Your children round me, grown,
Yet, twelve bright lustres trying to be true
Sixty years, they're all from You.
You've learnt, dear Sisters love Him too
Given life and love so true

(Sixty years of wild-eyed temper
From the outset to December,
All my failings you have gladly borne
Never left me all alone
T'is a miracle of patient faith
I'll be grateful unto death.
T'is a miracle of patient faith
I'll be grateful unto death)

Now, the years are swiftly passing
No new sixty years to Hope,
Somewhere in the coming morrows
Times will come, we cannot cope
Then His grace, His love still follows
Comfort for the years of pain
Strength of heart, now once again!

Sisters, we still work for Uva
Province blessed by tea and cane,
Let its tanks filled, overflow
Let its waving golden grain
Please the eye and deck the Table
As the hungry mouths are fed
Ease our pangs, let all be able
Work in harmony for Bread.

—Rodrigo, 1987.

5

Transformational Faith
Embracing Death for Justice

> "When the moment arrives, we must be prepared even to sacrifice our lives for the poor."
>
> —Rodrigo (undated).

ON A PHYSICAL LEVEL, Fr. Mike died a gruesome death. It was nothing short of the slaughter of the lamb. His execution revealed the depths of brutality that power and indifference could sink to. As Mahinda Namal[1] noted on the occasion of his twenty-fifth death anniversary, "In reality, his was a political assassination. From a faith perspective, it was martyrdom."[2] Even though he was physically felled by a bullet, his spirit has not been extinguished by any means. This gentle, extraordinary man encountered an

---

1. Sri Lankan liberation theologian.
2. Namal, "25 Years Ago," para. 3.

undeserved cruel end. Yet, his vision endures. His mission is replicated, and his quest is carried forward. Thus, on a symbolic level, it was a sanctified death—a blessed Passover to a peace that surpasses all peace, in the way that he had been theologizing for decades. It was the final and full moral Passover unto selflessness that was at the heart of his teaching. The mere fact that three decades hence, a vibrant discussion continues on his ideas, his vision, his quest, and his theology is ample testament to the fire of wisdom personified in him, a burning flame not extinguished.

Long before his untimely death on the night of November 10, 1987, Fr. Mike was known to have declared "only my bones will leave this place." He was referring to his deep love for the poor and the enduring spiritual connection he felt with them. This declaration also hinted at his protective instincts toward them that would continue beyond his physical existence. A testament to his words, after the tragedy that ended his life, his brain, heart, and eyes were buried on the compound of Suba Seth Gedera, symbolic of the most vital organs that had facilitated his keen observations and analytical acumen, his acute sensitivity, and deep empathy for the plight of the poor. The rest of his body was transported first to Dehiwela to the charge of his ever-loving family. Finally, he was in repose at Fatima church for viewing by the larger public. From there, a mournful procession of his extended family, friends, and parishioners who had loved, supported, and revered him accompanied him on foot to his corporeal resting place at Kanatte, the main burial ground in the city of Colombo.

The events of his last fateful night have been written and recounted by numerous lay and religious figures alike, who knew and admired him, and heralded him as a martyr for justice. The significance of his death lies in his willingness to sacrifice his life, his earthly/physical form, for the cause of justice, and his refusal to be consumed by fear, nor cower in the face of violence. The events culminating in his assassination have also been clearly recalled by the two nuns who had been working with him at SSG, and the people of the surrounding village area. This chapter documents the prelude to his assassination, the backdrop of political tension that prevailed in the mid-1980s in the country, and the underlying reasons why he was perceived as a threat, i.e., his outspoken critique of the economic exploitation of the poor in Buttala, his steadfast commitment to their upliftment, and his courageous efforts to question and confront the oppressive forces.

NONVIOLENT MEANS FOR JUSTICE

As a person well acquainted with the social and economic circumstances that had laid the foundation for the JVP[3] insurgency, Fr. Mike's primary concern was to discourage a resort to violent tactics, and to redirect the youth to focus on building their self-reliance. On his part, he had committed to providing material and moral support to strengthening their livelihood security and economic empowerment. In this undertaking, he found himself hemmed in by two extreme assertions of power. On one hand, he was confronted by the local power holders (including members of Parliament, government representatives, traders, and money lenders) who were puzzled by his motives and irked by his attempts to redress the injustices heaped on the poor in Buttala. On the other hand, he was similarly challenged by the JVP youth and sympathizers in the village who felt that his efforts were inadequate and that his tactics were not radical enough. As Fr. Tissa Balasuriya and others have documented, not only was he "considered a threat by the affluent and the powerful"[4] in the village area, but also by disenchanted groups of rural youth. For their part, the youth of the area had reached a point of sheer desperation and exasperation over their situation, after long years of being relegated to the social and economic margins of the society. The rhetoric of resorting to radical and violent means offered by the JVP leadership at the time appealed to them as the only way to wrest power away from the entrenched social and political hierarchy in Sri Lanka.

> Fr. Rodrigo advocated a nonviolent struggle for people's integral liberation. . . . Fr. Mike was not a Marxist. He understood the problems of the youth, though he did not share in their response and strategies.
>
> —Perera, "Editorial," 5–10.

> Sri Lanka cannot continue to hide its crying injustices for very long. Our very first option as men of goodwill must be liberation, the passing over. Rural people, students, youth in prison and out of it, all the oppressed must take up their own liberation. The whole nation will thus be conscious and morally alert for a complete break with economic and political imperialism.
>
> —Rodrigo, "Moral Passover," 8.

Fr. Mike was one of the handful of Christian leaders of the time who had decidedly taken a vocal and active stance for social and economic justice for the poor. He advocated securing social justice by inculcating the principles of

---

3. Janatha Vimukthi Peramuna (JVP), translated as People's Liberation Front, the militant movement for social justice formed by southern youth in Sri Lanka.

4. Balasuriya, "Fr. Michael Rodrigo OMI," 9.

> If a person does only social service such as helping to build wells and toilets, or running a school and health clinics, the affluent tolerate it. But when one gets to the stage of helping people to organize themselves peacefully, to obtain their rights, one runs in to difficulties especially with those who oppress the poor.
>
> —Balasuriya, "Fr. Michael Rodrigo OMI," 8.

self-help and self-reliance, as well as by engaging the poor to empower themselves and bring about social transformation through nonviolent means. He was prepared to risk his life for his commitment to this end goal of justice for the poor. He firmly believed that the poor of Buttala could work collectively to improve their quality of life in a sustainable manner. He carefully identified and meticulously documented the sources and forces of impoverishment in the area, and the contrast in living conditions between the rich and powerful and the downtrodden in society. He argued that "such structuring of society is highly unjust, unreasonable,"[5] and that the route to justice was through deeper spirituality, not merely in an inner/intellectual journey, but by engaging with the poor in an experiential process.

> Spiritual renewal can lead to a fresh approach to socio-political commitment and then concern for justice and solidarity will be an essential part of Christianity, a genuine dialogical experience.[6]

Fr. Mike's framework for undertaking such a dialogical experience was through the model of dialogue of life that he had put forward as a contextualized presence among the poor, representing and witnessing Jesus to them. As he clarified,

> Dialogue of Life is a more difficult experience than intellectual dialogue of scholars. This is particularly so at the village level. For here, one is at close quarters with the ongoing struggles of rich and poor, landlord and the landless, the money lender and the poor debtor, the officials and the public, the politicians and then people ...[7]

As the story goes, Fr. Mike's persistent efforts to bring justice to the poor was perceived as an inconvenient obstacle by the various individuals involved in corrupt practices. Thus, the many forces that opposed him colluded together to bring about his demise. His efforts to protest the violent methods used to arrest presumed JVP members in the village were

---

5. Rodrigo, "Example of Village Dialogue," 9.
6. Ibid., 10.
7. Balasuriya, "Fr. Michael Rodrigo OMI," 8.

interpreted as sympathy for the JVP. He was suspected of harboring the JVP cadre in the village who were presumed to be planning to overthrow the government through violent means. The late evening gatherings at SSG of JVP "boys," as they were referred to at the time, where Fr. Mike engaged in discussions with them about how to avert violent confrontations and explore peaceful reform strategies were misinterpreted as radicalizing sessions. His habit of intervening to object to the physical harassment and verbal abuse meted out to women (wife, mother, or sister of a JVP "boy"), even going so far as to entreat the army to mete out the punishment to him instead, was misunderstood as a pretext to protect the so-called offenders. Ironically, as noted above, there was initial skepticism and frustration even among the JVP youth with Fr. Mike's strategy for village empowerment. They were suspicious of his intentions and had confrontations with him, until with customary gentleness, extensive knowledge base, extraordinary skills as a teacher, and typical charisma, he was able to win them over. Summing up the challenges he faced from all sides, Fr. Mike had once commented, "The radical revolutionaries may also disapprove of 'reformist' measures and peaceful approaches."

BACKDROP

Irritation and resentment had been slowly brewing among a small group of influential individuals in the Buttala area with Fr. Mike's persistent efforts to document and report the pillage of rural resources and the exploitative practices that compromised the livelihood security of the poor. He had sent several personal letters to then-President J. R. Jayawardena over the course of the mid-1980s about the deplorable living conditions in the Buttala area, the political favoritism by local politicos, their bold efforts to thwart drought-relief payments due to those who were perceived to be political opponents, the actions of traders and merchants who felled the precious resources of virgin teak forests as local politicians turned a blind eye (because they were sure to have received a commission from the sale of the timber), etc. He regularly penned letters to the highest authorities in the State Timber Corporation about the latter travesty. When the opportunity presented itself, he invited foreign journalists and broadcast companies to document the appalling situation in the area. He also registered open protest against the exploitative labor practices of the adjoining Pelwatte Sugar Corporation (PSC), a joint venture between the government of Sri Lanka (which held 51 percent ownership of its assets) and Booker-Tate, a giant in the global sugar industry. He was transparent in identifying the specific figures responsible for the exploitative practices, including members of parliament. The practice by President Jayawardena was to forward the letters onto the respective individuals named by Fr. Mike. Presumably, the sense of humiliation and embarrassment caused to them prompted their efforts to eliminate him.

At a time in the history of Sri Lanka when excessive force, torture, and detention was sanctioned outright and unhesitantly resorted to by the army, a prevailing sense of fear and disbelief had virtually silenced the population. A special task force was formed by the government to weed out the so-called JVP insurgents. It resorted to random midnight raids in unmarked jeeps to abduct presumed JVP members at gunpoint. Sleeping youth were rudely awakened, accused of participating in insurgent activities, while mothers, sisters, or wives protested. They were then handcuffed, blindfolded, packed into a jeep with no license plate and rustled away.

Their tactics were brutal and repressive. They relied on deceptive ploys such as negotiating a lesser punishment if a suspect could identify another JVP member. Many a young man, unable to identify any such individuals, yet conscious of the fact that they would not be believed if they did not

Sri Lanka's Counter-Insurgency Campaign of the 1980s

In the late 1980s, as the nation battled the war for Tamil sovereignty in the north, the beleaguered government of then President J. R. Jayawardena agreed to the formation of a counter-insurgency campaign (COIN) to flush out the youth rebellion in the south. Charged with the task of rooting out youth affiliated with the JVP, para military groups resorted to the tactics of random targeting of rural areas to "search, interrogate, and destroy" presumed rebel youth. Small teams of counter-insurgency forces were deployed to the rural south to work under cover, and authorized to mete out extra-judicial killings. They were endowed with near-unlimited powers under the provisions of the state of emergency declared by the government. These death squads were masked, armed with automatic weapons and travelled mostly at night in unmarked vehicles. They resorted to trickery to identify JVP cadre, used brutal methods of torture upon capture, imposed harsh terms of detention and if confirmed as a JVP member, summarily executed, often after mutilation and beheading. Many innocent young men (and a few women) were detained and killed in this manner, including some who were falsely accused due to personal disputes, or family feuds over land or political allegiances.

As a way of discouraging rebel activity, the decapitated heads of supposed rebels were strategically placed at major landmarks (culverts, bridges, junctions), hung on lampposts and trees, and other visible locations. Bodies of supposed rebels were often dismembered and burned on a pyre of tires. These became common sights around the country in the late 1980s.

name someone, pointed the accusing finger at innocent others. Hundreds of rural youth, particularly from the Buttala area (then considered the hotbed of the insurrection) were captured in this manner by the armed forces, tortured with excessively cruel methods, and detained at camps such as Boossa, if they survived.

Regular visits by the army were common at SSG. The security forces deployed to Buttala and Kataragama (see map, p. 54) made frequent stops to question Fr. Mike about his purpose in the village, to warn him about sheltering rebel youth, and to challenge his perspectives. On these occasions, Fr. Mike made it a point to engage them in a discussion about the poor and the conditions of poverty that the villagers of Buttala lived under. His aim was to raise their awareness about the living conditions in the Buttala area, and the nature of economic injustice. It was to no avail. Ever suspicious of his true motives, the security forces subjected SSG to random searches, including and especially when they were following tips or rumors to hunt down a suspected insurgent. His tendency to intercede when village families were being unreasonably harassed contributed to the antagonistic stance the security forces had developed toward Fr. Mike, even while he maintained a demeanor of calm and equanimity. His habit of expressing chagrin at the use of profanity and corporal harm to mothers and wives by the security forces was also not well received by hardened security personnel bent on executing their mandate to root out the insurgents.

The forewarnings issued to Fr. Mike had been stepped up to the point that the security forces had even stopped by at the Theological Update event in Ampitiya, convened by the Oblate Ongoing Formation team in August of 1987, to caution Fr. Mike to leave Buttala, a mere three months prior to his execution. Yet Fr. Mike was undaunted in his decision to stand with the people and not abandon them at that critical moment. Sadly, it was an era when the assassination of a lone priest in a remote village at the social and economic margins of the nation could be easily executed, justified, and even dismissed as a casualty of the times. Even the Catholic Church found itself helpless in pursuing the investigation of Fr. Mike's death as it was confronted by appalling accusations of two sorts: one that claimed his murder was due to his colluding with JVP boys, and the other that pointed the accusing finger at the JVP as the perpetrators. The fact that Fr. Mike himself had grown increasingly unpopular within the church as he took a stand with the poor and exhorted the church to undertake a radical self-examination had created an aura of ambivalence about his true intentions.

Many who admired and endorsed Fr. Mike's convictions found the stance taken by the church not to press for an indictment entirely unfathomable.

PRELUDE

The days leading up to the fateful event had been tension filled, as Sr. Benedicta and Sr. Milburga recall. Rumors circled around the village that Fr. Mike and the community at SSG were being targeted for an assault. There was much talk between the sisters and other residents of SSG about what

> "Greater love has no man than this, that a man lay down his life for his friends."
> —John 15:13.

course of action to follow, given their deep concern for Fr. Mike's safety and wellbeing. On several occasions they had tried to persuade him to leave SSG at least temporarily until the situation had settled down and the looming threat to their work and Fr. Mike's life had eased. Fr. Mike's response was simply to surrender to the will of God. He continued to voice his love and concern for the people of Buttala, and his unwillingness to abandon them at that critical moment.

Details of the days preceding his murder recorded by the *Christian Worker*[8] offer a glimpse of how the stage was set for his elimination. The chain of events began on November 4, 1987, when a mudalali (businessman) named Mr. Madduma was shot at (but not killed, only injured) outside his home in Alukalavita village. Just before midnight that night, a dozen armed men in uniform claiming to be the police surrounded Suba Seth Gedera and called out to Fr. Mike. They pressed him about the whereabouts of the culprit, alleging that he was hiding Mr. Madduma's assailant. When he invited them in, they proceeded to search the residence with a flashlight (torch), given the lack of electricity at SSG, and rummage through his documents. Failing to find any incriminating evidence, they departed, only to return the next morning for further interrogation.

This time, they informed Fr. Mike that there were several petitions against him, presumably charging him with supporting the youth insurgents. Since Fr. Mike was aware of the individuals who were against his work with the poor, he named them and asked for confirmation. He also countered by asking them to get testimonials from others in the village about his work

---

8. Christian Worker, "Prophet, Priest and Martyr."

there. The armed group immediately quipped that the petitioners' charge was that JVP indoctrination classes were being held at SSG. Fr. Mike and the two sisters then proceeded to patiently clarify that the classes held at SSG were on literacy and agricultural training programs. Unconvinced, the armed men had retorted, "You are helping the JVP to hide." At that point, Fr. Mike had produced his files showing the names of the trainees. Still undeterred, the armed men made a bold assertion: "Those in hiding have connections with you. They have survived because of you. What is your connection with the people here?" Fr. Mike's unwavering response was, "As a follower of Jesus Christ, I have made an option for the poor. All of my connections are with the poor because they are poor. I am not interested in party politics."

They continued to pressure him, asking him to provide the names of JVP members in the village (a typical police tactic of the day with the intention of flushing out the JVP cadre). Fr. Mike's sardonic reply was that he could not know who the members were since the party was proscribed. Irked by this response, they pressured him further. "You will never help us. You are useless. Just give us one name." When he refused again, they issued a stern warning, forbidding him to allow any youth to visit SSG but for a few exceptions (possibly undercover agents), adding an ominous forewarning that it would reflect badly on him if JVP youth were to visit the premises. To this, Fr. Mike's response was a firm refusal to exclude anyone, and to further reiterate that it would be difficult for him to distinguish between JVP and other youth.

The very next day, on November 6, several armed men in uniform visited the village again, picked out one youth and packed him into their jeep, with a warning to others about being mindful of their actions. This put enough of a fright in the youth in the village to the extent that those who were regular visitors at SSG in the evenings refrained from gathering there from then on.

Four days later, on November 10, 1987, the same armed men visited SSG at noon and spoke in a civil manner with Fr. Mike for some time. He engaged them in a discussion about their religious beliefs and spoke to them about the dangers of militarization and the need for human values. Upon their departure that afternoon, the leader of the group cautioned Fr. Mike to abandon his mission in Buttala, and that he would see him again enroute to the Kataragama Temple, an important site of worship for Buddhists, Hindus, and indigenous communities alike in Sri Lanka (see map, p. 54). Despite the appearance of civility, this visit was not as innocuous as it seemed. Fr. Mike was gunned down that very evening.

> We are a part of the people and they must be consulted. I have consulted them and they are unanimous that we should stay. Otherwise they would have no one to turn to in their difficulties. For me the Voice of the People is the Voice of God. They have decided we should not leave them and that is the Voice of God for me. In any case I will not foist my opinion on anyone. If the Community decides otherwise, I will abide by it. After all my bones are light enough to be carried away.
>
> —Rodrigo, quoted in Christian Worker, *Father Michael Rodrigo.*

Unbeknownst to him, a command had been issued to the extra-judicial squads deployed by the state, referred to as the "Yellow Cats," to assassinate Fr. Mike. As recounted by Lambert (pseudonym), the villager on the adjoining property to SSG, "We in the village noticed the arrival of three 'strangers'[9] in our village, individuals toting guns. At some point, we learned that they were targeting Fr. Mike and the residents at SSG. That afternoon when Sr. Milburga was on her way to wash clothes at the river bank, several people in the village sounded a word of caution about these strangers and their ill intentions. I, myself, had a conversation with Sr. Milburga urging her to convince Fr. Mike to leave the village immediately. She then hastened with me on her heels to inform Fr. Mike that there was a credible report of a threat. I stayed back at the door while she conveyed this information to Fr. Mike. He immediately dismissed it and exhorted her not to listen to gossip. I felt helpless at that time, and a little annoyed that the information I gave was rejected. I returned home wondering what to do."[10] Fr. Mike's first response had been to surrender the decision to the Lord. According to Sr. Benedict, what transpired after Lambert had departed was that Fr. Mike had repeated his pledge that only his bones would leave Buttala, and urged everyone at SSG to pray.

He had then dropped to his knees and had prayed with arms outstretched for over an hour. His suffering was visceral, just as Christ's agony

> A shot rang out. My ears were blocked and I fell from my sitting position. I suddenly realised that I lay in a very uncomfortable position. I wanted to change my position but was afraid to stir fearing something further. We were all numb and remained in that condition for perhaps over half an hour until Sr. Benedict said in Sinhala 'Father ivarai' (Father is finished). I did not still understand until I saw Fr. Michael's brain lying on the floor near me, intact.... The skull broken to bits was lying on the floor, blood and pieces of flesh spattered the walls. All three of us too were soaked in blood. Sr. Benedict said: "Come and see, his blood is in the chalice."
>
> —Sr. Milburga Fernando, quoted in Christian Worker's Fellowship, "Prophet, Priest and Martyr."

---

9. Unknown individuals.

10. Personal interview, July 19, 2016.

was intensely palpable. He wept. According to Wijeyeratne, "As though in the grip of a premonition of his fate, Fr. Michael had, with overpowering anguish, intoned Psalm 130: 'Out of the depths I cry to you O Lord; Lord hear my voice!'"[11]

As evening grew and darkness gathered, he had invited the others, Sr. Benedict, Sr. Milburga, and Shirani (another devotee resident at SSG) to prepare for mass, two hours earlier than the usual time of 7 p.m. for the daily mass at SSG. As they talked among themselves, delaying assembling for mass, Fr. Mike proceeded to arrange the items for the mass himself. He then began singing the opening hymn solo as a way of drawing the others into the little chapel area at SSG. Seated in typical fashion on the floor with his back to a small window, he had announced at the beginning of the mass that they would also deliberate on the decision to stay or leave the village. He had distributed slips of paper with one side denoting the reasons for staying on, and the other side stating reasons for leaving so that each person could mark their choice.

The little faith community at SSG then proceeded with the mass, partook of communion and wine, and at some point reflected and prayed about the decision. According to Wijeyeratne,

> Bringing the service to a close, he had exhorted the members of the community in the following words, "After all, the lasting things are love and relationship with people. These things will last even in eternity. Don't be afraid, we will commit ourselves to God." As a closing prayer, he had stated, "Into your hands O Lord I commit my spirit."[12]

He had reiterated his stance clearly to the little community:

> Why should we be afraid to die? Witnessing (to the poor) does not mean escaping from the crisis. If we are needed by the people, we should not desert or abandon them. Now we shall surrender our lives to God.[13]

He had then bowed his head to pray about the decision, committing that and their lives to the Lord, and raised his right hand for the final blessing. A noise at the window behind him made him turn his head, only to be met with the assassin's bullet, fired at close range. He had slumped forward,

---

11. Wijeyeratne, "Harvest Dream," para. 9.
12. Ibid.
13. Christian Worker, "Prophet, Priest and Martyr."

his head shattered and brain matter splattered across the room, including the rafters. His blood had filled the chalice.

Thus ended the life of a courageous champion of justice. Nonetheless, his quest, his valiant struggle for justice did not end, despite his physical demise. As written in John 12:24–26, "Unless a grain of wheat falls into the earth and dies, it remains alone; but if it dies, it bears much fruit." Fr. Mike's death allowed for a broader awareness of the injustice of poverty and led generations of Christians in Sri Lanka to embrace the struggle for social justice. Christ himself was persecuted partly because he stood with those at the fringes of society. His mission was to redeem and align himself with the poor and marginalized. He chose not to be at the center of political power. Fr. Mike had grasped this truth early in his life and fulfilled Christ's mission through his journey for justice for the poor masses of Sri Lanka.

According to the Christian Worker, inquiries they made provided insights into those culpable for Fr. Mike's assassination.

> On the evening of Fr. Michael's murder two boys from the village who used to visit Suba Seth Gedera had been chased away by persons in uniform that evening before the shooting. According to these boys the two men in uniform who chased them away were in a vehicle parked about 200 yards away from Suba Seth Gedera. A villager had reported that a vehicle slowed down near Suba Seth Gedera that evening as if to drop someone off,[14] and had then gone some distance beyond and stopped. The vehicle had later returned, slowed down and left. A village girl cooking nearby that evening had said she had heard the sound of someone wearing boots running away from SSG around the time of the incident.[15]

---

14. Presumably the assassin.
15. Christian Worker, "Prophet, Priest and Martyr," 9.

6

Epilogue
Aftermath: The Voice Not Silenced

> Fr. Mike is the most Christ-like figure Sri Lanka ever produced. He is an excellent example of another Christ (*Alter Christus*). He is the Sri Lankan disciple of Christ par excellence.
>
> —Meemana, "Fr. Michael Rodrigo, OMI is at the Foot of the Cross," para 21.

EACH YEAR, ON THE anniversary of his death, the villagers in Buttala gather at SSG, bringing clay lamps filled with coconut oil to light wicks of twisted cotton, placed reverently in flickering rows along his burial site. Children adorned in auspicious white bring hand-made garlands of jasmine flowers that are draped over his grave stone. Tears are shed, requests are whispered for healing and hope. Stories of his self-sacrificing qualities and anecdotes of his jovial nature are retold. Around the island, masses are held in his honor and unfailingly at St. Mary's Church, Dehiwela (his home parish) and at Fatima Church, in association with the Centre for Society and Religion. Poems sing his praises, and newspaper articles extoll his virtues. The claim that "in his death the inarticulate and the powerless lost an effective voice" is contradicted by the multiple ways in which his legacy continues. Those whose lives he touched briefly or longer are irrevocably transformed in one way or another.

> The quality of Mike's witness and its impact on the people he served cannot however be disputed. When the Buddhist villagers found his dead body lying on the ground, they reverently gathered up the pieces of his brain and the eyes which had fallen out and buried them in the garden, putting up two crosses to mark the spots. In doing so they said, "these were the eyes which saw our condition and this is the brain that guided us. These were the most precious parts of his body and since we have them, Fr. Michael still remains with us."
>
> —Christian Worker, "Prophet," 1.

Apart from these annual remembrances, Fr. Mike's memory and legacy of sacrifice is honored in a number of other ways. Catechism books in Sri Lanka include a paragraph about his vision and work, seminarians who studied under him who have assumed key posts in the church hierarchy espouse his perspectives on serving the poor, and volumes have been published on Fr. Mike's theological insights. Thus, his voice has not been silenced, his efforts have not been in vain, and his vision for justice has catapulted him to a central spiritual role beyond his death.

> Even by dying every true martyr witnesses to the reign of God here on earth. In actual fact, authentic living and dying are inseparable. Authentic living is always towards a kind of martyrdom. No martyr's life is ever a waste. The blood of the martyr is the seed of God's reign. Every martyr is an ambassador of Christ. They represent the truth about God in the most profound manner.
>
> Fr. Mike died exactly the way he lived by emptying himself totally and offering himself utterly and generously. He died by creating a space for life. His living unto death was very life-giving. His death was another phase of his mission. His death was also part of his dynamic mission. Death is the moment of truth. Death is the hermeneutical key to a meaningful life. He got things right about what it is to become a follower of Christ in our crucifying world. He died because of his decisive and single-minded fidelity to the Kingdom of God. His whole life became a sacrament and an instrument of God's reign.
>
> —Meemana, "Difficult Vocation," 8–9.

DYING, HE CONTINUES TO LIVE

As Fr. Romesh Lowe (Ampitiya National Seminary) observed, posthumously, people have begun to recognize Fr. Mike's true quest, even though many failed to fully grasp the profound depth of his thought while he was alive. A significant development within the Oblate congregation and in many parts of the Christian community in Sri Lanka is his recognition as a martyr, and a movement to declare his martyrdom. As another champion of the poor and a leading figure in Sri Lanka's advocacy for social justice, the late Fr. Tissa Balasuriya observed,

> While the church is praying for peace and for a saint through the miracle of peace, we are presented with the witness of a martyr. Will the saints of our contemporary situation have to be martyrs due to their fidelity to the gospel and humanity? Those of us who have known Fr. Mike over a lifetime, and more intimately during the past few years have no doubt that his intention was to live, and if need be die, for the very poor people of our country, specially

of Uva, whom he loved so tenderly, inspired by both the Buddha and Jesus Christ.[1]

This chapter documents several ways in which Fr. Mike's legacy is alive: his theological impact across the Christian community in Sri Lanka, Asia, and beyond; transformations within the church in Sri Lanka; the ongoing work among the poor in Buttala; and the movement to call for his recognition as a martyr. I start with the latter first, the case for his martyrdom, given its paramount significance.

> "He endured a martyr's death for the cause of justice."
>
> —Fr. Mervyn Fernando, personal interview, July 14, 2016.

MOVEMENT FOR MARTYRDOM

> Fr. Mike, a dear friend, and authentic witness to the Lord and his Gospel, has been snatched so suddenly and so brutally from our midst, from the midst of the poor whom he loved so much. But his "spirit" will live on not only in his beloved people but as an inspiration to spur on thousands of others to opt courageously for the poor and the oppressed.
>
> —Fernando, "He Who Opted for the Poor," 52.

The term "martyr," originating from the Greek word, *martus*, which means "to witness," was used in the early church with reference to those who provided testimonials of Jesus Christ's death, burial, and resurrection (e.g., Acts 1:22). In its traditional use, the strict sense of martyrdom is applicable to those who are killed specifically for their faith beliefs. As Jesus proclaimed, "Whoever finds his life will lose it, and whoever loses his life for my sake will find it" (Matt 10:39). Jesus's beckoning thus was alluding to the *willingness* to lose one's life for His sake. Fr. Mike had already explicitly confirmed his willingness to die on behalf of the poor long before his assassination. He was known to have regularly stated, "When the moment arrives,[2] we must be prepared even to die for the people."[3]

The reasons Fr. Mike was eliminated is not as straightforward as "for his faith," as some have argued. It was more about how he enacted his faith, as a living witness to Christ, to Christ's core message for humanity, and in his choice of being present in Christ among the poor, especially in the

---

1. Balasuruya, "Fr. Michael Rodrigo OMI," 10.

2. May also be translated as "presents itself" (i.e., "When the moment presents itself").

3. Synonymous with the poor, in the tacit meaning of this word in the Sinhala language. Rodrigo, in a letter to his eldest sister Hilda, September 28, 1987. This was a mere forty-two days before his assassination.

face of flagrant violations of justice. Faith, for Fr. Mike was not something abstract, nor a mere concept in scripture or theology. It was a live, dynamic, lived out process. As his dear friend and collaborator Fr. Tissa Balasuriya noted,

> He lived his Christian, religious and priestly calling faithfully, following the footsteps of the Master, who too died a similar death. For him, the message of Jesus and Buddha was clearly calling him to be active alongside the exploited poor.[4]

Fr. Michael sacrificed his life, not for stubbornly defending dogmas of the Roman Catholic Church, but for living Christ in the intimacy of unshakeable faith: by motivating, energising, showing concern for and defending every human being irrespective of his faith.

—Wijeyeratne, "Harvest Dream," para. 10.

In this way, Fr. Mike vested his faith with far more energy and dynamism than mere words of encouragement or exhortation, or even scriptural utterances. He infused his faith with the zeal of sacrificial action that lies at the heart of Christ's mission for humanity. Thus, it is evident that Fr. Mike was killed because of his faithful living out of Christ's call to serve the poor, and to challenge the systemic injustices they were burdened by. He was felled by forces who failed to understand the core message of Christianity as redemption for the poor, spiritually, socially, and economically. Fr. Mike exemplified an unfailing commitment to the cause of uplifting the poor to the very end in his decision to remain with the people of Buttala. Standing by his decision not to abandon them under the political turmoil of the day, he had affirmed, "After all, my bones are light enough to be carried away."[5] In this way, Fr. Mike was prepared to, and did, as the Beatitudes beckoned, "Lay down his life out of love for others."

The recently martyred Blessed Romero (Archbishop Oscar Romero of El Salvador) offers an eerie parallel to the cause of martyrdom for Fr. Mike. Similarly felled by an assassin's bullet just eight years prior to Fr. Mike's death, Cardinal Romero was an outspoken critic of human rights abuses perpetrated by the repressive Salvadoran government, and spoke out on behalf of the poor and the victims of oppressive government practices. Fr. Mike was likewise forthright in his critique of exploitative practices,

---

4. Balasuriya, "Fr. Michael Rodrigo OMI," 9.
5. Christian Worker, "Prophet, Priest and Martyr," 8.

whether by government functionaries, multinational corporations, or local politicos. Like Oscar Romero, Fr. Mike named names—of local politicians, businessmen, their henchmen, and collaborators. He was known to have confronted local government representatives who withheld rations and financial allocations to youth in the village, simply because they had voted for the opposition party. He regularly reported their practices of harassment and humiliation of village youth and poor families. He wrote a string of letters to the national Timber Corporation about illicit felling activities by notable figures in the area. He regularly wrote to the highest authority in power, then–Prime Minister J. R. Jayawardena. This reportage subjected him to the ire of the powerful forces in the area who saw him as an obstruction to their ulterior motives. They were at once resentful and fearful of him—fearful of being exposed, resentful of what they perceived as his "meddling" in their affairs. They wanted him out of the way, so that they could continue to fleece the poor and exploit the natural resources of the area with impunity. He represented an obstacle to their base ambitions for profit. More significantly, his presence, his work, his commitments, and the spirit in which he worked to uplift the poor contravened their worldview.

His mere presence as a symbol of virtue was a persistent reminder of their corruption—an unsettling reflection of their debauchery. Eliminating Fr. Mike was in a way like shattering the tell-tale mirror of conscience. Fr. Mike's murder was thus also a psychic act of evading remorse, while its symbolic significance is in absorbing the ills of a nation that had grown complacent to the suffering of some, akin to the meaning embedded in Christ's willingness to die for the sin of the world.

> His life was sacrificed on the altar at which the sacrifice of Christ was simultaneously enacted.
>
> —OMI Mission, "Fr. Michael's Life Journey," para 5.

In many ways, Fr. Mike personified the ideas put forward by Blessed Romero with whom he shares some uncanny parallels. As Ashley clarifies, "Romero's spirituality of the preached Word included, *demanded* a concrete incarnation in his life and ecclesial practice."[6] This point was illustrated in a homily Fr. Romero delivered in 1978.

> It's easy to preach his teachings theoretically. To follow the pope's magisterium in theory is very easy. But when you try to live, try to

---

6. Ashley, "Oscar Romero, Religion and Spirituality," 122.

Epilogue

incarnate, try to make reality in the history of a suffering people like ours, those saving teachings, that is when conflicts arise.[7]

Like Fr. Mike, Blessed Romero had been incorporating biblical teachings in to his homily in a way that exposed the injustices around him. As Ashley notes, his words were meant to "vivify, enlighten, contrast, repudiate and praise what was going on in the country. And he did this precisely because of a deeper engagement with the suffering of the people in his church."[8]

> The violence we preach is not the violence of the sword,
>   The violence of hatred.
> It is the violence of love,
>   Of brotherhood,
> The violence that wills to beat weapons
>   into sickles for work.
>
> —Romero, *Violence of Love*, 14.

LOVE COMMANDMENT

One of Fr. Mike's oft quoted sayings is: "Love all equally and each one more than the other." He embodied Jesus' love commandment by practicing compassion for the poor, love for the vulnerable, and redemption for the oppressed. Like Archbishop Romero, he exemplified a deep love for the people, especially the rural poor, long oppressed at the callous hands of history and social hierarchy. Both were crusaders for social justice, a quest borne and carried out from the depths of their profound love for humanity. Archbishop Romero used the enigmatic phrase "the violence of love" to capture the contrasting force of brutal violence inherent in political subjugation with the passionate love for humanity, especially the downtrodden. He described this in his poem "Violence of Love" penned ten years before Fr. Mike's assassination (see above).

Clarifying what Archbishop Romero meant by this term, Pope Francis in his letter to the current Archbishop of El Salvador on the occasion of Romero's beatification spoke these words:

> It is necessary to renounce "the violence of the sword, of hatred," and to live "the violence of love, which left Christ nailed to a cross, which makes each person overcome their egoism and ensures that no such cruel inequalities are among us." He knew how to see and

7. Ibid., 122–23.
8. Ibid., 123.

experience in his own flesh "the egoism that lurks in those who do not want to give up themselves in order to reach others." And, with the heart of a father, he cared for "the most poor," asking the powerful to convert their "weapons into scythes for work."[9]

Like Blessed Romero, Fr. Mike was fierce in his love for the poor and in his confrontations with oppressive forces. Part of the text of the paper he presented at the religious conference in Berkeley, California, just months prior to his assassination capture his laments about the vast social inequities in Sri Lanka, as shown in the box to the right.

Rev. Oscar Romero used the phrase "flame up" to refer to the emotions he felt upon witnessing the dire poverty in rural El Salvador. Similarly, Fr. Mike used the Sinhala word "Kakkuma" to sum up that sensation of intense, burning fervor for justice for the poor that he experienced in the depths of his being. The literal translation of the Sinhala word "Kakkuma" is an "ache," which one may impute as a force that emanates from deep within the person, i.e., the bowels (of compassion). It was what Fr. Mike understood as the source of compassion. In attempting to illuminate that source of compassion, he was known to have reiterated, "Jesus had compassion for the people. Compassion does not come from the mind or the heart. It comes from our very bowels." This was his way of clarifying that compassion, the acting out of empathy was almost at once an instant and instinctive response from the inner being, the "gut," and not something one mulled or deliberated over. He would have also drawn upon the word for compassion in Sinhala, his native language, "Anukampava," which is a fusion of two intimations: "anu" to refer to a feeling extended to another, and "kampava" to refer to tremendous inner turmoil. The extent of tumult connoted by this word is best understood when one considers that it, together with the word for earth in Sinhala, "bhumi," connotes the turbulence of an earthquake (i.e., bhumi-kampava). It captures the immediacy and immensity of the compassionate response upon encountering

> Those raking in the surplus and the unseemly profits live in places, large dwellings vaunting vulgar affluence; drive in limousines while the vast masses have just stepped out from a stalled bus—unroadworthy bus on unbusworthy roads—in rank rural areas of Asia. While the few enjoy higher education and read the high literacy rate charts in the capital city, literally millions drop out from school at an early age. The few dominate, dictate, control, cajole, the others are suppressed, cowed into submission, victims of threats, thugs, force, despair.
>
> —Rodrigo, "Example of Village Dialogue," 9, para. 5.

---

9. Francis, "Pope Francis' Message," para. 5.

Epilogue

the suffering of others, as the parable of the Good Samaritan illustrates. It entails no hesitation, no momentary pause, nor inner deliberations to weigh the options. In like manner, compassion was instantaneous and second nature to Fr. Mike. It was the source of his actions of mercy and selfless love for those suffering unjustly.

> In dying by a bullet of those who stood against his own nonviolent presence and appeal to conscience, human decency and social justice, he has certainly died in a manner he may have had a premonition of—a martyr to the cause of the poor and the voiceless, whose destiny's inaudible murmur he held hope.
>
> —Fernando, "Fr. Michael, Man of Dialogue," 14.

ANTI-POVERTY ACTIVIST

It is easy to surmise that Fr. Mike was incensed by the indignity of poverty. His engagement with the poor was rooted in his desire to restore their dignity, their basic human rights, and their quality of life. In this sense, he was a fiery anti-poverty activist. He was a staunch supporter of social equality and decried the structural forces that trapped the poor in a vicious cycle of poverty. Cognizant of the historical factors as well as the social and systemic dynamics that constrained the livelihood options of the rural poor, he made a choice to join them at the margins of society—in what is tantamount to a "bottom up" approach to poverty reduction.

He opted for social transformations from the ground up, rather than top-down, partly because he astutely realized that the top down approaches were not only paternalistic, hence replicating the disempowerment of the poor, and ineffective, if not nonviable. Based on this author's discussions with Fr. Mike in early 1987 during my doctoral field research in the area, I can attest to his extensive familiarity with international development theory and the body of literature critiquing some of its questionable premises and outcomes. For example, he was highly critical of the formula of foreign direct investment, based on the evidence from the operations of the Pelwatte Sugar Corporation (PSC) in Buttala. Since his arrival in the area, he had been documenting the dispossession of the rural poor from their land as a result of

> It was a case of living with the people, living with the poor, for these peasants were the neglected groups of the remote Bintenne. He worked with them for village upliftment in a small way, by schemes of self-help herbal medicine, organic manure systems, better nutrition for the children, care for school drop-outs, assistance to build toilets and wells, etc.
>
> —Forbes, "Commemoration," 32.

PSC,[10] the selective employment opportunities,[11] and the lack of decent work conditions,[12] as well as the negative environmental effects[13] of large scale, commercial sugar cultivation. His focus was on restoring the livelihood security of the people of Buttala.

Leading anti-poverty scholars and activists, such as the anthropologist and medical doctor Paul Farmer,[14] have argued that poverty is inextricably intertwined in the way power operates in a society, creating the conditions for structural inequalities. Such inequalities are embedded in the privileges and dis-privileges associated with social position and are manifested in inequities instituted in the structures of society, which restrict access to resources, services, and opportunities. These inequities are reinforced over time and across society through asymmetrical power relationships and the indiscriminate exercise of power in brutal ways. The renowned Indian economist and anti-poverty advocate Amartya Sen notes, for instance,

> "How tragic," he had said, "if discovering the eternal law of love, one cannot speak of this, or show of this in daily life to another so that we may both work towards the fulfillment of human destiny."
>
> —Fernando, "Fr. Michael, Man of Dialogue," 14.

> The asymmetry of power can indeed generate a kind of quiet brutality. . . . Inequalities of power in general prevent the sharing of different opportunities . . . inequality of power in different forms, is central to deprivation and destitution.[15]

---

10. Many in the farming communities adjoining Buttala were ousted from their land, often given meager compensation and cajoled to settle on plots allocated by PSC where they were expected to grow feeder sugar.

11. As documented in his letter to President J. R. Jayawardena, jobs in the factory or in the fields were reserved for political favorites, with local politicos interfering in the selection of candidates as well as their omission.

12. According to the International Labour Organization (ILO), decent work includes, at a minimum, safe work conditions (including provisions to safeguard worker health), fair and equitable wages, secure terms of employment, benefits such as sick leave, and reasonable hours of work (to ensure adequate rest during the work day). These criteria were rarely met at PSC. See Gunewardena, "Bitter Cane," for a detailed discussion of the working conditions and their negative repercussions for the rural poor in the area.

13. For example, contamination of ground water with the sulfide residue from the sugar factory, acres of land cleared that not only meant deforestation but also altered elephant migration routes, to name a few.

14. Farmer, *Pathologies of Power*.

15. Sen, "Foreword," xvi.

Epilogue

As an erudite scholar, Fr. Mike was acutely aware of the specific structural forces operant in rural Sri Lanka that were a source of disempowerment and disprivilege for the poor. Fr. Mike relied on his in-depth understanding of the roots of social inequalities, its dynamics, the structural mechanisms that perpetuated it generation after generation, as well as the sustainable routes to exiting poverty in his work with the poor.

Although he knew that policy shifts were essential for meaningful change in the conditions that kept rural Sri Lankans mired in poverty, he opted for building self-reliance among the poor as a far more sustainable strategy. In the words of Rev. Vianney Fernando, Bishop of Kandy,

> He opted to be with them to support them in their struggles. Above all he understood the deepest meaning of his ministerial priesthood as taking on the "Servanthood of the Kingdom" following his master and savior Jesus Christ. When threatened by forces that militate against such an option, he carried on undaunted.[16]

Equally remarkable was Fr. Mike's emphatic insistence on a participatory approach to poverty alleviation, now heralded as a cornerstone of sustainable poverty reduction efforts.[17] As his close friend and collaborator, Fr. Dalston Forbes had noted, "His work was an intimate partnership with the village people."[18]

All the programs he initiated were in consultation with the villagers, even in the case of much needed programs that provided essential services. For example, he first sought the consent of the people even to hold a clinic day at SSG, a weekly event to treat a variety of ailments as part of the health outreach program run with the expertise of Sr. Benedict Fernandopulle.

Furthermore, he eschewed the grand development strategies[19] advocated by the government in power, knowing full well that these were moti-

---

16. Fernando, "He Who Opted for the Poor," 51.

17. See, for example, Chambers, *Whose Reality Counts*; Cornwall, *Beneficiary*; and Mohan, "Participatory Development," on the emergence of participatory development approaches in the 1970s as the antidote to top-down strategies, in an effort to ensure their sustainability by instituting "buy in" and a stake in the development process by the poor. Participatory development is now accepted as common wisdom in any program that recognizes the right of the people to shape their destiny, in recognition of their inherent right to determine the direction and terms of their economic and social empowerment.

18. Forbes, "Commemoration," 32.

19. For example, the entire policy of the "open economy" that was a hallmark of President J. R. Jayawardena's government, which has subsequently been traced to many of Sri Lanka's development deficits, especially in terms of the quality of life.

vated more by national political ambitions and could result in further disempowerment of the poor of Lanka. As learned as he was, he could have opted for efforts solely on the policy front, which would have certainly made his life easier. Yet, partly in keeping with the Oblate mission to serve the poor directly, and partly because of his own convictions about working hand-in-hand with the poor, he chose the latter, more difficult path. As Sarath Fernando of the Devasarana Development Centre noted, he had made a "clear decision to remain with the poor, continuously helping them to understand the reasons for their situation and also the potential they had to overcome this situation."[20] As such, Fr. Mike was that rare anti-poverty activist who lived his convictions in a way that immersed him in the daily suffering of the poor, beyond the intellectual exegesis of theorizing on poverty.

> He saw their deep suffering; how the development process had largely left them by, unattended. He combined a concern for them with his search for a "dialogue of life" as he called it, between Buddhism and Christianity. Living among a wholly Buddhist population, he worked with Buddhist monks to alleviate the sufferings of these people. He helped them to improve their conditions of life and their understanding of society and its processes.
>
> —Balasuriya, "He Paid the Supreme Price," 12.

Interestingly, it was his identification with the poor that leads us to understand the complex nature of his commitment—embedded in an abiding love and compassion for the poor. "This is where I belong, my home is with the poor," he was known to have stated often, despite the regular invitations to international conferences, the prestigious offer to become a part of the faculty at the Institut Catholique in Paris, and the string of invitations to give talks, lectures, and sermons from around the country as well as across the Asia region.

Fr. Mike's steadfast concern for the poor seems to have arisen from the depths of his being, a sensation that could only be summed up as a burning ache that consumed his very being, similar to Oscar Romero's term "flame up."[21] This inflamed sense of compassionate love called for a greater conversion on the part of Fr. Mike, who had not grown up in poverty like Cardinal Romero. Fr. Mike made a crucial physical as well as spiritual transition from the life he had known in opting for the poor, in his journey as an

---

20. Fernando, "Vision and Mission," 23.

21. A term Archbishop Romero used in a conversation with Cesar Jerez, the Jesuit Provincial Council of Central America in the 1970s, in order to explain the inner turmoil he experienced. See Ashley, "Oscar Romero, Religion and Spirituality," 124.

anti-poverty activist. He left behind the comforts of the seminary and the protected confines of the church, which had afforded him the middle-class amenities he was accustomed to. He had no reservations about entering the harsh terrain of rural life shared with the poor in all its manifestations—the inhospitable landscape of the Dry Zone in which Buttala is situated, bleak eco-climatic environment, a deeply stratified and exclusionary social structure, and a highly divisive, abusive, and corrupt political climate. He embraced with joy the inordinate challenges he faced and the difficult conditions under which he carried out the work of economically and socially empowering the poor.

The conditions of poverty were intimately familiar to Oscar Romero, as he acknowledges in a 1975 interview. "I was born into a poor family. I've suffered hunger. I know what it's like to work from the time you're a little kid."[22] Yet, once he joined the seminary, his life improved and it was only after twenty-three years of being a parish priest when he was sent to the poverty stricken area of Santiago de Maria that he witnessed poverty again. By contrast, Fr. Mike hailed from a middle-class family and was unfamiliar with the situatedness of poverty as a living reality until he observed it through his efforts to contextualize the liturgy during his teaching years at the Ampitiya National Seminary and subsequently at the Sevaka Sevana seminary in Badulla. These encounters with the poor led to a rare, profound, and visceral transformation in his understanding of their condition. This we may consider as the very embodiment of a love so great that it was of cataclysmic proportion. In the words of Br. Jude Lal Fernando, "His zeal as a Christian to join the struggle of the poor masses and thereby be a partner in building up of church for the poor never ceased."[23]

Despite all the challenges he faced, Fr. Mike always registered a tremendous sense of joy in his service, as many who met him recall. Although he lived in the sparsest of conditions, under the threat of violent retaliations, he did not perceive his mission in Buttala as a drudging sacrifice. He undertook his work not through a sense of obligation, but more because his heart was moved to act, and the actions he took on behalf of the poor gave him a sense of sublime satisfaction, equating it to the work of love in Christ.

---

22. López Vigil, *Memories in Mosaic*, 158.
23. Fernando, ""Fr. Michael Rodrigo and His Contribution," 102.

PACIFIST

As a pacifist, Fr. Mike vehemently opposed violence, and was outspoken in his critique of the indiscriminate violence used by the army and security forces against the youth, as well as women in the Buttala area and around the country. In his discussions with the youth, he was known to have repeated a foundational Buddhist teaching in the *Dhammapada*,[24] quoted in Sinhala, *"Vairayen, vairaya nosansindeth"* ("hatred is never appeased by hatred, but by love alone"). Similarly, he engaged the armed forces in discussions about faith and nonviolence, emphasizing their foundations in both Buddhism and Christianity. He worked tirelessly for economic justice as the route to peace, based on the rationale that it was not merely the political and social marginality that had prompted the formation of the youth insurgency, but also the sheer frustration of rural youth upon seeing all avenues for advancement in life foreclosed to them in the prevailing hierarchical social and political structure. In his letter to President J. R. Jayawardena, dated March 11, 1986, he reported,

> My view is that it would be a very nice idea to have all the Youth working together, content, satisfied that the village area can find them jobs and job-satisfaction. Irreligion is of no use. So, we have induced youth to hear the moral word.[25]

As one commentator noted about Blessed Romero, he "was martyred because he faithfully followed, without fail, in the steps of Jesus in choosing decisively to side with the victims of injustice and violence."[26] In like manner, Fr. Mike denounced the injustices he witnessed—the injustice of economic depravity, the injustice of dispossession (of land) and displacement, as well as the injustice of political persecution. Like Cardinal Romero, Fr. Mike was vocal about the suffering endured for generations by the rural poor in Sri Lanka, and was unflinching in bringing the attention of government authorities to the individuals and corporations responsible for these atrocities. He resorted to the use of the pen, letters regularly written about the excesses of influential political figures and traders in the area who were engaged in illicit felling of timber and other lucrative but illegal activities that jeopardized the livelihoods of small-holder farmers in the Buttala area.

24. The *Dhammapada* is the collection of Buddhist scriptures that have captured the most important sayings of the Buddha.
25. Rodrigo, "Letter to President."
26. Wright, "Reflection," para. 3, line 4–7.

Epilogue

He appealed to the moral reasoning of government authorities, especially calling for wisdom to prevail, alluding also to the possibility that higher level government authorities may not be aware of the injustices occurring at the rural periphery, and forewarning of the tendency for private vendettas carried out behind their backs, as evident in his closing comments in the letter to President Jayawardena.

> Social justice, ahimsa (nonviolence) and interreligious dialogue were all integral to his work. While social groups were involved in the struggles of life, he presented constantly the path of justice and nonviolence. He did so always with a selfless manner, with understanding and compassion towards all.
>
> —Balasuriya, "He Paid the Supreme Price," 12.

> May I hope and pray, Your Excellency that the hour is not yet too late. Violence, even if it comes from disillusioned youth, can be stemmed if wiser counsels prevail in these areas, and not if empty-headed officials who hold non-gazzetted posts are allowed to wreak their private vengeance on an unsuspecting government.[27]

As noted in chapter 5, he regularly intervened when the army resorted to brutal beatings of the family members of suspected insurgents, begging the officers to beat him instead. Time and again, Fr. Mike boldly demonstrated how he was prepared to sacrifice his life for the vulnerable.

ALTRUIST

Fr. Mike chose his path, his journey for justice, instinctively. Consumed with a passion for restorative justice, he thought little of the risks and the costs to himself. It was a response to what stirred in him upon witnessing the pathos of poverty in rural Lanka. Although it entailed a conscious choice, a planned process, and purposive action, it was prompted out of an inner conviction that he must act, that he must take redemptive action, action to render social justice. Obviously, as a learned person, and as one well versed in the liturgical principles and theological advances of the day, Fr. Mike was thoroughly familiar with the leading ideas of Catholic social teaching of the 1970s, such as liberation theology. Yet, his choice of immersing himself in the *practice* of those theological constructs, by leaving the confines of the church and yielding to the hardship of the wilds, so to speak, attests to something intrinsic to his nature. That something we may

---

27. Rodrigo, "Letter to President."

deduce is the rarest form of human compassion—the wellspring of *altruism* (clarified in the commentary in the box below), that irrevocably overrides the human tendency to act in one's self interest.

Fr. Mike thus can be considered a genuine altruist in the way that Monroe (1996) clarifies altruism as "a sense of shared humanity, a perception of self at one with all mankind."[28] He perceived the impoverished of rural Sri Lanka as Christ sees them—through tender eyes of love and compassion, and an intrinsic bond of common humanity that bound him to them, a characteristic that is attributed to innate altruism, stemming from a universalistic worldview. According to Monroe, altruists tend to have a "perception of themselves as one with all humankind."[29]

> Altruists have a particular perspective in which all mankind is connected through a common humanity, in which each individual is linked to all others and to a world in which all living beings are entitled to a certain humane treatment merely by virtue of being alive.
>
> —Monroe, *Heart of Altruism*, 206.

Monroe further argues that "ethical political action emanates primarily from one's sense of self in relation to others."[30] The sense of a shared humanity with others that she alludes to has been demonstrated by Fr. Mike, as with Blessed Romero. That perception of a common humanity is thus the impetus to take action on behalf of the other, even at the risk of one's life, as Monroe argues, evidenced in Fr. Mike's sacrifice of self. Contrary to the premises of rational choice theory, which posits that actors simply act in their self-interest, altruism operates in a global sense, on the rationale that any act of inhumanity to another diminishes the self. However, an important caveat is operant in the case of Christian compassion, which is not merely aroused through the conscious awareness of ethical action. This is the key to understanding the kind of altruism displayed by one such as Fr. Mike—informed by his role as a Christian and a priest, and not merely out of a sense of obligation, but through the lens of total empathy and love that prompts the urge for restorative justice.

> Tell me, what is the real meaning of "Buddhuvenava" (becoming a Buddha)? I think it is to do what you are doing here: to see to the sick and distressed.
>
> —D. Karunapala, quoted in Rodrigo, "Example of Village Dialogue."

---

28. Monroe, "Heart of Altruism," 206.
29. Ibid., 204.
30. Ibid., 217.

Epilogue

TESTIMONIALS: THE FRUITS OF THE SEED

Jesus Christ was the divine-made-human example of the fruits of the spirit: love, joy, peace, long-suffering, gentleness, goodness, faith (Gal 5:22). These were the qualities that Fr. Mike aspired for, emulated, and encouraged in others. The fruits of the seeds planted in all these ways are manifested in the lives of the villagers he worked with, as their testimonials below reveal. Fr. Mike's endeavors in Buttala were two-fold: for the moral and spiritual development of the youth and children, and for their economic empowerment. Now in their fifties and sixties, the youth who had benefitted from those efforts offer testaments to the guidance he provided in their positive character formation and preparedness for the job market. Villagers continue to talk about Fr. Mike's good work and their continual striving to make the younger generations aware of all that he did (see testimonials in appendix).

> When he died, the spontaneous appeal rising from the hearts of all sections of the people of Buttala was: "We want that presence to continue." The graceful presence of Father Mike in their midst which touched every dimension of their lives was perceived by the people as the "Good News," the "Coming of the Kingdom." This certainly is the ultimate goal of every Missionary and every Disciple of Christ.
>
> —Samarakone, "Trail Blazer," 95.

DIALOGUE OF LIFE CONTINUED

Since his untimely passing, the work to empower the poor launched by Fr. Mike has continued, despite some ebbs and flows. Suba Seth Gedera has been renovated after a lapse of a few years following his death when the original clay and stick structure began to disintegrate. Key programs he initiated such as the preschool, the English classes, and the herbarium are being continued. These ongoing programs at SSG stand as a firm testament to Fr. Mike's open arm policy of welcoming the stranger and sister, the destitute and delinquent. SSG remains as a symbol of his love for the poor, his witnessing of Christ to the poor. Most importantly, it attests to Fr. Mike's enduring legacy of redemption for the oppressed in rural Sri Lanka.

Equally significant is the outcome of the various programs he launched, in terms of improving the lives of the rural population. Tearful acknowledgements are made of the literacy and English competency gained by youth in the village, most now middle aged. Those who benefited from his tutorials in preparation of their final exams (referred to as A-levels in the British system of education followed in Sri Lanka) are cited as holding decent jobs and sustainable livelihoods. In a tangible manner, the coconut seedlings program Fr. Mike launched has resulted in hundreds of well-established coconut trees that offer shade, building material, and food as well as income for the villagers.

> Everyone who showed a genuine love for the people would always live in their hearts. Therefore, what we feel is that Fr. Michael of Suba Seth Gedera is ever present among us, the poor peasant masses of Alukalavita, and he has not gone away from us. Though he had to sacrifice his life untimely, because he acted with honest dedication for justice, he would live eternally in the hearts of the poor and those who aspire to renew this sad face of the earth.
>
> —Herath, "Fr. Mike of Suba Seth Gedera," 91.

"Each time we pluck a coconut and eat from it, we remember Fr. Mike and his generosity, his warmth, and his untiring efforts to improve the quality of our lives," remarked one villager, now in his late fifties. "We recall his noble qualities, his efforts to guide the youth to follow a wise path in life," remarked another. "The children who grew up during Fr. Mike's time here in the village benefitted a lot from his work. They are now adults who are gainfully employed," another observed, adding that "even every second of our lives, we silently express our gratitude to Fr. Mike."[31]

THEOLOGICAL LEGACY: DENIAL OF SELF, DEPLORING POVERTY

The most important aspect of Fr. Mike's theological legacy is his elucidation of the poor as representing Jesus Christ, in a cosmic sense. "Jesus is the poor and the poor is Jesus" he was known to have insisted. He maintained that truth was to be found with the poor. Moreover, as Stuckey notes, "Following Pablo Richard, he maintains that the poor are the human authors of the Bible. The Bible is the "subversive memory of the poor."[32] His prolific writing on the subject of working with the poor attests to his conviction that "discerning Christ in the poor"[33] and working in the service of the poor was at the heart of his calling.

---

31. Personal interviews with villagers, July 2016.
32. Stuckey, "Dialogue of Life," 79.
33. Rodrigo, "Hope of Liberation," 191.

Epilogue

More profoundly, beyond a mere witnessing of presence in Christ to the poor, Fr. Mike understood Christ's calling as one that required an unconditional denial of self. He clarified that such a renunciation was "Jesus' example of self-emptying (kenosis in Phil 2)."[34] He linked this self-denial to the Buddhist notion of detachment.

> This leads us to the spirit of detachment, release from the bonds of goods and consumerism; it will induce groups to live as did the first Jesus community, the original church of those called by him to go and sell what they had, give to the poor and then follow him.[35]

Taking the calling one step further, Fr. Mike also understood this process as culminating not merely in renunciation, but also *denouncement* of poverty, as clarified by Fr. Romesh Lowe (personal conversation, July 2016). Denouncing poverty entailed speaking out against the roots of oppression and exploitation in the quest for social justice. "Jesus made a preferential option for the poor,"[36] he had noted in one of his last public presentations. Elucidating how that option was the reason for Christ's untimely and unjust death, Fr. Mike indicates that it was "because he stood for the human, he fought for the poor."[37] He perceived such a defense of the poor as inherent to Christ's calling, and that being prepared to accept the grim risks associated with taking up that calling was part and parcel of the process. "The following of Jesus demands that we also defend what he defended. In this we risk death ourselves."[38]

> It is our contention that our being present to the poor peasant here is also our being present to the Christ who identifies himself in some secret way with the poor.
>
> —Rodrigo, "Hope of Liberation," 190–91.

Finally, he emphasized the role of the Christian church in advocating for human rights, spelled out in a Vatican working paper:

> In continuing the prophetic mission of her founder, the Church must more forcefully preach and realize more effectively this liberation of the poor, the outcast and the worker working with others, building with others a world where every man, no matter his race, religion or nationality can live a fully human life, freed from

---

34. Ibid., 195.
35. Ibid.
36. Ibid., 194.
37. Ibid., 195.
38. Ibid.

servitude imposed upon him by other men or by natural forces over which he has not enough control.[39]

From beyond the brief span of his earthly life, these words echo as a vibrant legacy of Fr. Mike's urging to the rest of us, especially the Christian Church.

THE WAY FORWARD: SAMVĀDA: THE FUTURE OF INTERFAITH DIALOGUE

> May the greatly respected and venerated memory of Fr. Michael keep alive the thirst for justice, peace and brotherhood among all people of goodwill and firmly establish the belief that peace, which is the fruit of justice and fraternity, can be achieved in our time if only we are truthful and sincere and are committed to pursue it.
>
> —Fernando, "Message," 13.

One key endeavor inspired by Fr. Mike's vision and engagements in social justice is Samvāda, a Sri Lankan Catholic journal of interreligious dialogue, owned and published by the OMI community. Launched in 2012 under the guidance of Rev. Fr. Rohan Silva, the OMI director for Colombo Province, this journal aims to honor his legacy and to continue his idea of engaging interfaith exchange through an active, responsive dialogue. Spearheaded and achieved through the editorial leadership of Fr. Claude Perera,[40] a key Oblate theologian, the stated purpose of Samvāda is to serve as a launching pad for a conversation with other religions, with the ultimate objective of furthering consensus, mutual understanding, and respectful tolerance of differences.

Now available online, Samvāda serves as a platform for interfaith dialogue. The first issue includes a Festschrift honoring Fr. Mike. Subsequent volumes explore a range of issues, including Fr. Tissa Balasuriya's influence on the theological developments in Sri Lanka, recent paradigm shifts in interfaith dialogue grounded in indigenous and vernacular conceptual frameworks, parallel motifs between Buddhist parables and those in the Old Testament, and critical analyses of concerns such as economic globalization. The most recent volume reiterates a fundamental truth that Fr. Mike espoused as a cornerstone of his engagement with the rural poor of

---

39. Ibid., 194 (quoting Pontifical Commission, "Justitia et Pax," 23).

40. Currently chaplain, University of Colombo at Peradeniya, and professor, Aquinas University.

Lanka: "Dialogue has a different modus operandi; namely those engaging in dialogue being equal partners having equal dignity and rights."[41]

MEMORIAL ERECTED FOR FR. MICHAEL RODRIGO

In 2001, exactly fourteen years after his demise, the Asian Human Rights Commission (AHRC) together with the Centre for Society and Religion (CSR) laid the foundation stone for a memorial of Fr. Mike in the Katuwapitiya area of Negombo. The memorial is intended as a reminder of Fr. Mike's vision and as inspiration for continuing his legacy of commitment to the poor, his tolerance, and profound respect for diversity.

THE VOICE OF THE POOR, A VOICE FOR THE VOICELESS, A VOICE WITH THE POOR

Voice is a powerful right, a basic human right. It assures the claim for rights. Yet, when systems and structures are in place in a society to rob people of that basic right, the claim for rights can take a violent turn. It is this truth that Fr. Mike understood, as the source of the anger behind the youth insurrections of Sri Lanka. Not that he condoned the violent methods in any way, but his empathy for the poor paved the way for his ability to comprehend deeply their railing against systematic social injustices. Fr. Mike's intention was not necessarily to become a voice for the poor and voiceless, but rather to *make space* for the voice of the poor to be heard, for their aspirations to be registered, for their dreams and hopes to be realized. As such, he also understood the drawbacks and limitations of representation and opted instead to work as a voice *with* the poor—to articulate their grievances, while paving the way for their empowerment. Evidence of Fr. Mike's impact on registering the voices of the poor on the national consciousness is in the intensified outreach efforts to the poor by the Catholic Church in Sri Lanka, and especially the efforts of the Oblate community.

ARRIVING AT JUSTICE

Fr. Mike's life entailed a long journey for justice for the downtrodden and oppressed. Although he was well versed in theories of social justice, the tenets

---

41. Perera, "Editorial," 5.

of human rights conventions, and the scholarly frameworks of social deprivation as the premise of economic marginality,[42] he relied more on Christ's teachings about justice. He was steadfastly focused on transforming the unjust structures of society that kept the cycle of hunger and poverty in motion. He was faithful to Jesus' mission to restore the humanity of those at the margins of society, to alleviate hunger, redeem the oppressed, befriend the outcast, and protect the helpless. He remained firmly anchored in the belief that restoring the dignity and hope of the poor was the route to balancing the scale of justice, and that ushering justice called for levelling the lopsided (often blatantly corrupt) systems biased against the poor and the vulnerable. It was because of his ardent advocacy and activism in all these respects that he, himself, was persecuted. He did not simply advocate for reforming the prevailing structures and processes that constricted the poor. He rallied the poor to become active participants in challenging the systems of oppression and transform them. Thus, he came to be perceived as a threat to the status quo of economic and political power that had a stranglehold on the geopolitical periphery of Sri Lanka. It is for these reasons that he was eliminated. Yet, those responsible for his death have still not been brought to justice.

> But the island was gradually being engulfed by violence, as an increasingly dictatorial and divisive government shut off opportunities for democratic dissent, driving many towards rebel groups which, in turn, terrorised hapless civilians. Much has been written about the "ethnic conflict," but many of the killings were of Sinhalese by Sinhalese, or Tamils by other Tamils.
>
> While the military killed rebel fighters and civilians unlucky enough to be in the line of fire, state-sponsored paramilitary squads detained, tortured, assassinated or "disappeared" suspected dissidents. Some Sinhalese youth joined the Janatha Vimukthi Peramuna, which at the time sought to overthrow the government by violence.
>
> —Hensman, "Amid Sri Lanka's Poor," para. 10–11.

At the time of Fr. Mike's assassination, in the absence of a careful investigation by the government and the police, a story circulated conveniently accusing the JVP of having carried it out.[43] However, the eyewitness accounts and the tell-tale boot print just outside the window from which the gun was aimed at him contradicted that rumor. Although the JVP had access to arms, it was widely known that they had little in the way of other military supplies

---

42. Sen, *Idea of Justice*.

43. Ironically, a list of the individuals put together by the armed forces that the JVP is accused of having eliminated includes Fr. Mike's name. See http://www.tchr.net/civil_and_pol_jvp_army_deserters.htm.

Epilogue

such as boots, and village boys accused of JVP involvement were typically barefoot due to their dire poverty. As the Catholic Church feared broader reprisals in the tension-filled political climate of the time, there was no effort made to press for an inquiry or probe into the cowardly act of gunning down an unarmed religious figure. Fr. Mike's family members were too engulfed in their sorrow to pursue such a course of action. A climate of fear prevailed across the country given the plethora of paramilitary groups, goon squads recruited by political figures, and the sweeping violent measures adopted by the security forces. Nonetheless, individual journalists and independent justice workers did not allow the matter to rest.

> Fr. Mike was moving ahead of his times in his thinking and praxis concerning People's power. He was clearly in the mainstream of history in opting for the people. We owe him a debt of fidelity and honour to keep his memory bright and burning and to develop his teaching on the Power of the people.
>
> —Forbes, "Commemoration," 34.

One individual in particular has been delving in to the records kept by the national Criminal Investigations Department (CID). A devoted Christian and deeply committed to social justice, he has shared the following details of his findings with the author. Approximately three years after his murder, a story surfaced of an unnamed army major subjected to a court martial for recruiting an assassin to gun down Fr. Mike. A parallel event led to a surprising discovery. The one medical doctor at the district hospital in Moneragala was treating a young soldier with psychosis. Not unheard of, due to the trauma of the violent events of the time witnessed by members of the armed forces, this particular young man was known to have repeatedly shouted out in anguish, "It is me, I killed him, Fr. Mike." With no possibility for recovery, the soldier was eventually discharged into the care of his family. Independent journalists who became aware of this story had visited his hometown, and managed to get a brief interview on his deathbed, including the identity of a high-level government official who had ordered the assassination of Fr. Mike. These details are included in this volume in the belief that a necessary part of arriving at justice in Sri Lanka is justice for Fr. Mike's brutal assassination.

CONSCIENCE OF THE NATION

The inspirational life of Michael Paul Rodrigo, priest, poet, and ardent practitioner of social justice, was truly a testament to the liberative truth of Christ's message to humanity. In his reflections and writing, he strove to illuminate a transformative understanding of Christ's summons to each of us, to become engaged in the making of a more humane society, according to what he understood as "the messianic expectation of the people . . . the victory or vindication of God's justice over evil in history."[44] In his letters, publications, sermons, and discussions, he bemoaned the inhumanity in Asia, and vividly described the suffering of the socially and economically dispossessed in Sri Lanka. Simultaneously, in his personal engagement in empowering the poor and voiceless, he served as the conscience of the nation. Just months prior to his demise, he had prophetically written, "While peace prizes reach some, others get only the bullet, depending on whether remote causes of exploitation and oppression are left aside or raked up."[45] His charge to Sri Lankans of all faiths is outlined in a call from the 1971 Synod of Justice (clause 51) that he emphasized in his last theological presentation.

> In the developing countries, the principal aim of education is for justice, and it consists in an attempt to awaken consciences to a knowledge of the concrete situation and in a call to secure a total improvement; by these means the transformation of the world has already begun.[46]

Everyone leaves behind their footprints in the sands of time, but only a few leave them bold and clear. We shall remember Fr. Michael Rodrigo and continue to love him as a man in whom the love of God and humanity always burned as a pure white flame.

—Dilan Perera, "Martyr of Our Time," 3, para 2.

---

44. Rodrigo, "Hope of Liberation," 209.
45. Ibid., 206.
46. Ibid., 196.

Appendix

Testimonials[1]

"With Fr. Mike's coming, Buttala experienced a new beginning, a new birth—the dawn of a new life. Perhaps he had to give up much to settle down in the village, for he was highly intellectual, with two doctorates. What a contrast! Soon he was one among us. His lifestyle was as simple as ours. His food exactly the same as ours. He was clad in a sarong and shirt, the simple garb of the people. He spoke and associated with us as one of us, so much so that he could speak directly to our hearts. He truly imbibed what was profound in the spirit of the people. What an honor to us! His thought patterns and actions were steeped in deep human values of compassion, care, concern: metta, mudita, karuna, upekkha as we call it. He witnessed to the deep truth that we all belong to the one human family of brothers and sisters, without any discrimination or distinction of class, caste, religion, race, social, or political standing. . . . What an example, not only for us, but for the whole world!"

—Deepika Herath, quoted in Fernando,
"Fr. Michael Rodrigo OMI," 23–24.

"Michael Father[2] drew in the youth of the village to focus on higher goals in life. He did so with kindness and love. For one, he constantly talked with

---

1. Except as otherwise cited, the testimonials were derived from the author's personal interviews.

2. Villagers habitually referred to him as "Michael Father" in accordance with the Sinhala language linguistic custom of role placement after the proper noun.

us about the path of peace and wanted to set us on a virtuous[3] direction. He arranged vocational training for groups of boys, helped the youth prepare for their A-levels, and gave us English lessons."

—Lahiru, sixty years old, village youth,
Alukalavita village, Buttala, Sri Lanka.

"Michael Father's main goal was to take the poor forward. It is because of him that the village has developed to this level. I was able to learn my letters[4] only because of him."

—Asitha, thirty-one years old,
Alukalavita village, Buttala, Sri Lanka.

"Michael Father tried to develop this area as a self-reliant area, to return it to the thriving state it was before the destruction of the Vellassa incident."

—Kumari, fifty-eight years old,
Alukalavita village, Buttala, Sri Lanka.

"Michael Father helped improve the state of our lives. He found a way for each house to get toilets. Before that we used to go into the bush. He distributed coconut seedlings, and thriposha. He travelled by bicycle or foot from house to house to get all the work done. He got us girls to join him in these programs. I was only thirteen years old when Fr. Mike arrived. He arranged for me to get training on health care delivery. After that special training, Sr. Benedict showed me how to dress wounds. I started working in the sugar cane fields at a young age to earn some money for my family. I have eight siblings. As soon as I finished my shift at 3 p.m. I would go directly to Suba Seth Gedera to help Sr. Benedict with the people who came to get medicine. She was the one in charge of the herbarium and she often used herbal medicines like *eramusu, polpala, kohomba*. We would work together until 9 p.m."

—Heen Manika, forty-five years old,
Alukalavita village, Buttala, Sri Lanka.

---

3. The word used in this comment was *yahamaga* in the Sinhala language, which literally translates as "virtuous direction."

4. Reference to literacy, and the preschool established by Fr. Mike (previously nonexistent in the village).

Testimonials

"There was an organic farming system started at Suba Seth Gedera upon Michael Father's initiative. No pesticides were used. Sr. Benedict was responsible for this too."

—Anonymous commentator,
Alukalavita village, Buttala, Sri Lanka.

"Michael Father was one of those extraordinary individuals who had such devotion for the people, the poor. He had so much compassion[5] for anyone. His heart melted[6] for anyone in need. He assisted every poor household in this village."

—Anonymous commentator,
Alukalavita village, Buttala, Sri Lanka.

"Whatever Michael Father did, it was in a jovial[7] manner. He lightened our mood. But, of course, it was clear that he was such an educated man. He was so wise and intelligent."[8]

—Anonymous commentator,
Alukalavita village, Buttala, Sri Lanka.

"Michael Father introduced an herbal garden at each of the four temples along with a water pump. A young girl from the village was appointed to manage each garden, and paid a small stipend of Rs. 250 per month. He started savings schemes for all the youth working on the herbal gardens and the organic farm."

—Wilbert, sixty years old,
Alukalavita village, Buttala, Sri Lanka.

"I started attending the classes at Suba Seth Gedera when I was fifteen years old. I was a school drop-out, and at that time, I just didn't have any motivation, nor the means to go to school. But, Michael Father took over all the drop-outs and taught us. He took us for vocational training, and I learned

5. *Anukampava*
6. *hitha unuvuna*
7. *vihiluven*
8. The exact term this person used was *Buddhimath*, which signified a combination of wisdom and intelligence in the Sinhala language.

Appendix

welding as a skill. Father also enrolled me in a driving school at Wellavaya where I learned to drive a bus. He even supported some of the youth to enter university. He treated us as if we were his own sons."

—Gunesekera, fifty years old,
Alukalavita village, Buttala, Sri Lanka.

"Because of Michael Father, the village gained a greater awareness of the issues in the village, in the country and how to conduct ourselves. I learned some valuable lessons from Michael Father—to discern between right and wrong, how to conduct myself in society, how to interact with others in a civil manner, how to undertake a task and finish it diligently to completion. He planted good things in our minds. He helped us develop personal character."

—Gunesekera, fifty years old,
Alukalavita village, Buttala, Sri Lanka.

"He used to advise youth who were accustomed to smoking and drinking. At that time, there were no taverns or anything like that, but people brewed *kassippu*[9] and sold it illegally. People drank mostly because of economic or interpersonal problems, not for entertainment. We felt a terrible sadness[10] and heartache[11] when we heard about Michael Father's murder, because of the amazing support he gave us. People were heartbroken when we learned that he had been killed."

—Gunesekera, fifty years old,
Alukalavita village, Buttala, Sri Lanka.

"The death of Michael Father is a terrible loss to us, to all of us, to the village. He used to advise those who erred. Whatever disputes arose, he invited the two parties to come over and discuss it. He was so patient and understanding with the youth. Even if someone did something wrong, or became angry with him when corrected, he never broke the relationship. He had a way of calming us down, and always used humor to guide us."

—Gunesekera, fifty years old,
Alukalavita village, Buttala, Sri Lanka.

9. Illicit brew made out of the sap of the coconut flower or fermented sugar cane
10. *dukha*
11. *vedanava*

Testimonials

"Michael Father was very close to the villagers. He took meals with us and the youth gathered at Suba Seth Gedera to talk to him. Even the JVP boys used to visit and discuss the problems of the area with Father. That is probably why he was suspected of supporting them. But, the fact of the matter is, Father Michael only tried to convince them to live in peace. He taught us the tenets of Buddhism.[12] He accompanied us to the temple. He always tried to protect us."

—Gunesekera, fifty years old,
Alukalavita village, Buttala, Sri Lanka.

"I was about sixteen years old when Michael Father came to this village. Initially, he invited me to help out with the preschool. I supported the work at the preschool. I also took English lessons with him. The first sentence he wrote on the blackboard spoke to the heart of our condition as young girls, and his purpose in uplifting our village: 'I have no protection. I hide in the shadow of the banana grove to bathe.' He understood the vicissitudes of our lives, he perceived the suffering we experienced. To start with, he researched what obstacles we faced. He worked with us through his compassionate heart. He became a village figure—got accustomed to our rough lingo. He adapted to an arduous[13] life here. He taught us self-reliance. More than anything, he developed our minds."

—Malani, fifty-five years old,
Alukalavita village, Buttala, Sri Lanka.

"I cannot capture in words how invaluable he was. Such a learned and righteous man, yet, such a down-to-earth person. He could understand anyone. He would not allow anyone to harm one of us in the village. He became like a god to us. In any predicament, Father came forward to help us. Suba Seth Gedera became a source of protection[14] for us, and for me in particular after the army killed my husband and dismembered him in front of my children."

—Malani, fifty-five years old,
Alukalavita village, Buttala, Sri Lanka.

12. *Buddha dharma*
13. *katuka*
14. The exact term used was *Rakavarnaya*, while the gist of her meaning was in the sense of a shelter or sanctuary.

Appendix

"We lived at that time in a condition of near servitude. We were a village that was prey[15] to exploitation. It was like a dark cavern. Michael Father changed that. He guided us to shape a new direction. It is too painful to discuss. It was he who raised our awareness. He labored on our behalf, walking from house to house to learn about our situation, and to distribute books, pens, roof thatching. He worked with us to dig wells in our back yards and community wells. There aren't enough words to capture the service rendered to us through Suba Seth Gedera."

—Nimal, fifty-two years old,
Alukalavita village, Buttala, Sri Lanka.

"Each time I pass this place, I remember Michael Father. We had nothing and he helped us understand our rights—our human rights. He died on our behalf. He remains forever in our memory.[16] He is beloved to us from the depths of our hearts. I often feel as if he is alive amongst us. He always strove to guide us on a good path in life."

—Nimal, fifty-two years old,
Alukalavita village, Buttala, Sri Lanka.

"I joined the work programs of Suba Seth Gedera in 1983. I taught in the preschool. Initially, I was a bit hesitant because I was unsure of myself. Michael Father then told me, 'What if I support you?' So, I agreed. He found a plot of land in the village to set it up. He was insistent that it should be a part of the village and not of Suba Seth Gedera. He wanted it to be *our* village endeavor. At that time, it was a clay and mud structure with a thatched roof. In 1986, it became a more sturdy building. Father arranged for the young girls who were interested in teaching there to get teacher training in Jaela and Kegalle towns, followed by additional training at the Moneragala *Mahila Samithiya*.[17] On opening day, he handed me the key and said, 'Nanda, you must stay here and continue this preschool until your old age.' I didn't want to break his word even though it became financially difficult for me to continue the preschool. So, in time, after his death, I took on the night shift when a garment factory opened in the town and worked in the

---

15. *goduru*

16. The exact term used was *Amaraneeya*, which refers to "deathlessness"—that he is immortalized in their memory.

17. A chapter of the national Women's Association.

school during the day until new teachers were recruited. Those children who grew up during Michael Father's time in this village and attended the preschool are now gainfully employed. Many entered the university and they advanced in life as a result."

—Nanda, age unknown,
Alukalavita village, Buttala, Sri Lanka.

"All that he did was a tremendous service for us. Because of him, our childhood was protected. He had some beautiful ideas. We honor him and the path he took. We remember him always and thank him every second of our lives."

—Nanda, age unknown,
Alukalavita village, Buttala, Sri Lanka.

"We never had a chance to travel beyond this village. He made that happen. He also set up a library and thus brought the world to us. He raised our consciousness—that we haven't lost even though we lost him. We will never forget that. He taught us self-reliance. He used to say, 'If you plant a mango seed, you own the tree. It is better than taking a mango from someone else.'"

—Somadasa, age unknown,
Alukalavita village, Buttala, Sri Lanka.

"At the start, a few young people were watching you carefully: 'How will you act towards us?' 'Did you come to turn us to your ways somehow?' or 'Were you an international spy group or spy ring to eventually sell out our village?' These were the questions which harassed us young people. But we went beyond mere observing and worked with you in our humble efforts as you worked with our people. There we discovered the true face of what you call sabhava, the Church."[18]

"I now see after all these years and for the last year especially, that this little Christian group—all of you—have understood our sorrow, our plight (*dukvedana*) and are really very loving and compassionate toward our people, especially the poor. Despite objections of a few who dislike the poor, the work of three of you has gone on. It is a valuable service: to rescue and

---

18. Rodrigo, "Hope of Liberation," 201.

teach the drop-outs, to supply what is wanting in the school schemata as regards certain subjects, to help adults in nonformal education; in short, to give us a hand. By assuring continuity of a reasonable distribution of infant food (*triposha*) from the government; by helping in a clinic day program, seeing to primary health care with a team of barefoot nurses drawn from our own village, and now working with a wider field of fourteen villages or so of this area; by helping self-sufficiency in agricultural inputs; by training ten farmers to do research and have technical advice on local fertilizer (bio-fertilizer) according to traditional methods, thus showing you want our culture to advance, and so you honor our happy past. We also have had, due to you, training in culture and dance items for the less-skilled but eager, and we have had slide-shows, which really have helped us live. You helped us with a library of 400 books and now, a 3,000 coconut plant scheme. It is for the poor. All this proves the true meaning of Suba Seth Gedera, the name of your house, 'Good wishes house.' You wish us well and want our true good. There is a new awakening among us, a renewal."[19]

"The example of this Christian group will never be forgotten by the growing ones of the village. To the Christian churches at large and to other religions, this is an immense example and a challenge. If, in this way, and with this background, every village could have such a course of action, a new light will dawn. Of this I am certain. Only then will village peace spread throughout the land. Then, an intelligent, wise, and exemplary people will arise in our country. The people will have a consoling, happy life."[20]

---

19. Ibid., 202.
20. Ibid., 202–3.

Bibliography

Ashley, J. Matthew. "Oscar Romero, Religion and Spirituality." *The Way* 44 (1995) 113–33. http://www.theway.org.uk/back/442Ashley.pdf.

Balasuriya, Tissa. "Fr. Michael Rodrigo OMI., Prophet and Martyr." *Logos* 27 (1989) 3–10.

———. "He Paid the Supreme Price of Love." *Centre for Society and Religion Pamphlet* 25 (1987) 12–13.

Benedict XV, Pope. *Maximum Illud*. Libreria Editrice Vaticana, 1919. http://w2.vatican.va/content/benedict-xv/it/apost_letters/documents/hf_ben-xv_apl_19191130_maximum-illud.html.

Boff, Leonardo. *Faith on the Edge: Religion and Marginalized Existence*. San Francisco: Harper and Row, 1989.

Boff, Leonardo, and Clodovis Boff. *Introducing Liberation Theology*. Maryknoll, NY: Orbis, 1987.

Brohier, Ralph L. *Ancient Irrigation Works of Ceylon*. Translated by L. Piyasena. Colombo, Sri Lanka: Mahaweli Authority of Sri Lanka, 1935.

Brohier, Richard L. *The Golden Age of Military Adventure in Ceylon: An Account of the Uva Rebellion, 1817–1818*. Colombo, Sri Lanka: Plate Limited, 1933.

Caspersz, Paul. "Priesthood, Poesy and Prophecy." *Logos* 27 (1989) 15–18.

Ceylon Today. "Fr. Michael Rodrigo OMI, A Priest of the Poor," n.d. (Article no longer available online or print.)

Chambers, Robert. *Whose Reality Counts: Putting the First Last*. London: Intermediate Technology, 1997.

Christian Worker's Fellowship. *Father Michael Rodrigo: Prophet, Priest and Martyr*. Colombo, Sri Lanka: Christian Worker's Fellowship, 1989.

———. "Prophet, Priest and Martyr." *The Christian Worker* 11 (2001). (Article no longer available online or in print.)

Cornille, Catherine. *The Impossibility of Interreligious Dialogue*. New York: Crossroad, 2008.

———, ed. *Many Mansions? Multiple Religious Belonging and Christian Identity*. Maryknoll, NY: Orbis, 2002.

Cornwall, Andrea. *Beneficiary, Consumer, Citizen: Perspectives on Participation for Poverty Reduction*. Stockholm: Swedish International Development Cooperation Agency, 2002.

Dharmasena, S. "Appreciation: Priest, Hero and Martyr of the Poor." *The Sunday Leader*, December 7, 2012. http://www.thesundayleader.lk/2013/12/07/fundamentalism-then-and-now/.

BIBLIOGRAPHY

Farmer, Paul. *Pathologies of Power: Health, Human Rights, and the New War on the Poor.* Berkeley: University of California Press, 2005.

Fernando, Augustine. "Fr. Michael, Man of Dialogue." *Centre for Society and Religion Pamphlet* 25 (1987) 13–14.

Fernando, Basil. "A True Practitioner of Conscientization," *Social Justice* 176 (2002) 18–22.

Fernando, Jude Lal. "Fr. Michael Rodrigo and His Contribution to the Christian Church." *Logos* 27 (1989) 96–109.

Fernando, Milburga. "Fr. Michael Rodrigo OMI, as We Knew Him." *Samvada* 1 (2012) 20–37.

———. *Harvest Dreams of Fr. Mike: Coming to Fruition.* Colombo, Sri Lanka: Centre for Society and Religion, 2010.

———, ed. *The Legend That's No Mere Legend but Challenge to Do the Truth in Love: Collection of Essays Dedicated to Fr. Mike.* Colombo, Sri Lanka: Center for Society and Religion, 1989.

Fernando, Reid Shelton. "Fr. Mike, Prophet and Martyr of Modern Sri Lanka." *Asia News*, July 14, 2012. http://www.asianews.it/news-en/Fr.-Mike,-prophet-and-martyr-of-modern-Sri-Lanka-25284.html.

Fernando, Sarath. "The Vision and Mission of Fr. Michael Paul Rodrigo." *Logos* 27 (1989) 19–24.

Fernando, Vianney. "He Who Opted for the Poor." *Logos* 27 (1989) 50–52.

Fernando, Winston. "A Message from Right Rev. Dr. Winston Fernando, S.S.S., Bishop of Badulla." *Samvada* 1 (2012) 11–13.

Forbes, Dalston. "Commemoration of Fr. Michael Rodrigo, OMI." *Logos* 27 (1989) 29–34.

———. "A Martyr for Social Justice." *Centre for Society and Religion Pamphlet* 25 (1987) 11–12.

Fowler, James W. *Faith Development and Pastoral Care.* Philadelphia: Fortress, 1987.

Francis, Pope. "Pope Francis' Message for Romero Beatification." *Super Martyrio*, May 23, 2015. http://polycarpi.blogspot.com/2015/05/pope-francis-message-for-romero.html.

———. "Pope: We Must Be Forthright in Interfaith Dialogue." *Catholic Herald*, January 13, 2015. http://www.catholicherald.co.uk/news/2015/01/13/pope-francis-speech-to-inter-religious-meeting-in-sri-lanka/.

Fredericks, James. "*Many Mansions?*: Multiple Religious Belonging and Christian Identity (Review)." *Buddhist-Christian Studies* 25 (2005) 167–70.

Gunewardena, Nandini. "Bitter Cane: Gendered Fields of Power in Sri Lanka's Sugar Economy." *Signs* 35 (2010) 371–96.

Gutierrez, Gustavo. *The Power of the Poor in History.* Maryknoll, NY: Orbis, 1983.

Harris, Elizabeth J. *Buddhism for a Violent World.* London: Epworth, 2010.

———. "Double Belonging in Sri Lanka: Illusion or Liberating Path?" In *Many Mansions? Multiple Religious Belonging and Christian Identity*, edited by Catherine Cornille, 76–92. Maryknoll, NY: Orbis, 2002.

———. "Tissues of Life and Death: Selected Poems of Fr. Michael Rodrigo, OMI." *Quest* 95 (1988) 1–88.

Hensman, Savi. "Amid Sri Lanka's Poor: The Life and Death of Michael Rodrigo." *Ekklesia*, November 16, 2012. http://www.ekklesia.co.uk/node/17394.

Herath, Madura. "Fr. Mike of Suba Seth Gedera (On Behalf of the Sorrowing Masses of Buttala, Who Weep Over Your Loss)." *Logos* 27 (1989) 87–91.

Bibliography

Hettiarachi, Kumudini. "Church with a Miraculous Beginning Celebrates 175 Years." *Sunday Times*, January 30, 2011. http://www.sundaytimes.lk/110130/Plus/plus_11.html.

John XXIII, Pope. *Mater et Magistra*. Encyclicals: Libreria Editrice Vaticana, 1961. http://w2.vatican.va/content/john-xxiii/en/encyclicals/documents/hf_j-xxiii_enc_15051961_mater.html.

———. *Princeps Pastorum*. Encyclicals: Libreria Editrice Vaticana, 1959. http://w2.vatican.va/content/john-xxiii/en/encyclicals/documents/hf_j-xxiii_enc_28111959_princeps.html.

López Vigil, Maria. *Memories in Mosaic*. Translated by Kathy Ogle. London: Catholic Agency for Overseas Development, 2000.

Lowe, Romesh. "The Word-Crucified in the Theology of Aloysius Pieris, SJ: Pieris' Contribution to the Development of a Christian Theology of Religions in the Context of Sri Lanka." PhD diss., Saint Paul University, 2012.

Meemana, Anton. "A Difficult Vocation: Fr. Michael Rodrigo, OMI at the Foot of the Cross." *Samvada* 3 (2014) 8–16.

———. "Fr. Michael Rodrigo, OMI, is at the Foot of the Cross." Unpublished essay, commemorating 24th death anniversary, 2014.

———. Untitled account. In *Daily Mirror*, October 25, 2011. (Article no longer available online or print.)

Mendis, Derrick. "An Appreciation." *Logos* 27 (1989) 40–42.

Mohan, Giles. "Participatory Development." In *The Companion to Development Studies*, edited by Vandana Desai and Robert B. Potter, 131–36. London: Hodder Education, 2014.

Monroe, Kristen R. *The Heart of Altruism: Perceptions of a Common Humanity*. Princeton: Princeton University Press, 1996.

Namal, Mahinda. "25 Years Ago: Assassination of Fr. Michael Rodrigo, OMI." Bapa's Space, December 28, 2012. http://ermomi48.com/2013/01/07/remembering-the-martyrdom-of-fr-michael-rodrigo-omi/.

Nyanatiloka, Bhikkhu, ed. *Buddhist Dictionary*. Colombo, Sri Lanka: Frewin, 1972.

Obeyesekere, Gananath. "Colonial Rape of Uva-Vellassa: Is History Repeating Itself?" Federalidea.com, July 24, 2007. http://www.federalidea.com/focus/archives/79.

O'Malley, John W. *What Happened at Vatican II*. Cambridge: Harvard University Press, 2010.

OMI Mission. "Fr. Michael's Life Journey." Unpublished manuscript. Rome: Archives of the Missionary Oblates of Mary Immaculate, 1–4.

———. "Michael Rodrigo—Dialogue as Mission." OMI Mission, July 20, 2006. http://mission-omi.blogspot.com/2006/07/michael-rodrigo-dialogue-as-mission.html.

Panabokke, C. R., et al. *Evolution, Present Status, and Issues Concerning Small Tank Systems in Sri Lanka*. Colombo, Sri Lanka: International Water Management Institute, 2002.

Parker, Henry. *Ancient Ceylon*. London: Lucas, 1907.

Perera, Claude. "Editorial." *Samvada* 1 (2012) 5–10.

Perera, Dilan. *A Martyr of Our Time*. Unpublished Manuscript, n.d.

Perera, Ranjith. "For a Younger Disciple." *Centre for Society and Religion Pamphlet* 25 (1987) 14.

Perera, S. K. "Message at the Funeral Service of Fr. Michael Rodrigo." *Logos* 27 (1989) 11–13.

Bibliography

Phan, Peter. "Multiple Religious Belonging: Opportunities and Challenges for Theology and Church." *Theological Studies* 64 (2003) 495–519.

Pieris, Aloysius. *An Asian Theology of Liberation.* Maryknoll, NY: Orbis, 1988.

———. "Christ Beyond Dogma: Doing Christology in the Context of the Religions and the Poor." *Louvain Studies* 25 (2000) 187–231.

———. *God's Reign for God's Poor: A Return to the Jesus Formula.* Kelaniya, Sri Lanka: Tulana Research Center, 1999.

———. "To Be Poor as Jesus was Poor." *The Way* 24 (1988) 186–97. http://www.theway.org.uk/back/24Pieris.pdf.

Pinto, Leonard. "Sri Lanka, a Brief History of Christianity." *Scoop*, September 22, 2013. http://www.scoop.co.nz/stories/WO1309/S00362/sri-lanka-a-brief-history-of-christianity.htm.

Pontifical Commission. *The Church and Human Rights.* Vatican City: Vatican, 2011.

Rittenbaugh, John. "Balanced Doctrine and Application." Sermon delivered October 2, 1999. http://www.bibletools.org/index.cfm/fuseaction/Audio.Details/ID/540/Unity-Part-5-Ephesians-4-B.htm.

Rodrigo, Michael. "Beginnings of Suba Seth Gedera," File no. 67, unpublished notes. Collection, Center for Society and Religion.

———. "An Example of Village Dialogue of Life." Paper presented at interreligious conference, Buddhism and Christianity: Toward the Human Future, Berkeley, California, 1987.

———. "The Hope of Liberation Lessens Man's Inhumanity: A Contribution to Dialogue at Village Level." In *Asian Faces of Jesus*, edited by R. S. Sugirtharajah, 189–210. Maryknoll, NY: Orbis, 1993.

———. "A Lamp to My Feet." n.d. Collection, Center for Society and Religion.

———. "Letter to President J. R. Jayawardena." Unpublished, March 11, 1986.

———. "Marginal Comments on Our Mass." n.d. Collection, Center for Society and Religion.

———. "The Moral Passover: From Self to Selflessness in Christianity and the Living Faiths of Asia." PhD diss., Institut Catholique de Paris, 1973.

———. "Notes Prepared to Guide a Group of Devotees Visiting SSG for a Religious Retreat." Unpublished, n.d. Collection, Center for Society and Religion.

———. "Pray with the Church." n.d. Collection, Center for Society and Religion.

———. "Some Aspects of the Enlightenment of the Buddha: In the Light of Principles of Knowledge and Being as Explained by St. Thomas Aquinas." PhD diss., Pontifical Gregorian University, 1959.

Romero, Oscar. *The Violence of Love: The Pastoral Wisdom of Archbishop Oscar Romero.* Edited and translated by James Brockman. San Francisco: Harper and Row, 1988.

Samarakone, Joseph A. "The Trail Blazer." *Logos* 27 (1989) 92–95.

Schubeck, Thomas L. *Liberation Ethics: Sources, Models, and Norms.* Minneapolis: Fortress, 1993.

Scott, James C. *The Moral Economy of the Peasant: Rebellion and Subsistence in Southeast Asia.* New Haven: Yale University Press, 1976.

Sen, Amartya. *Development as Freedom.* Oxford: Oxford University Press, 1999.

———. "Foreword." In Paul Farmer, *Pathologies of Power: Health, Human Rights, and the New War on the Poor*, xi–xix. Berkeley: University of California Press, 2005.

———. *The Idea of Justice.* Cambridge: Harvard University Press, 2009.

Bibliography

Silva, Rohan. "A Message from Very Rev. Fr. Rohan Silva, OMI, Provincial of the Oblates of Mary Immaculate, Colombo Province, Sri Lanka." *Samvada* 1 (2012) 18–19.

Singarayar, Philip. "Martyr in Living the Interreligious Dialogue." In *Oblate Missiologists*, edited by Harry E. Winter, 23–24. Washington, DC: Oblate Center for Mission Studies, 1997.

Stuckey, Thomas. "Dialogue of Life: Michael Rodrigo's Theology and Ministerial Formation." In *The Legend That's No Mere Legend but Challenge to Do the Truth in Love: Collection of Essays Dedicated to Fr. Mike*, edited by Milburga Fernando, 69–84. Colombo, Sri Lanka: Center for Society and Religion, 1989.

Sugirtharajah, R. S. *Asian Faces of Jesus*. Maryknoll, NY: Orbis, 1993.

Teicher, Jordan G. "Why Is Vatican II So Important?" National Public Radio, October 10, 2012. http://www.npr.org/2012/10/10/162573716/why-is-vatican-ii-so-important.

Tennent, James Emersen. *Christianity in Ceylon*. London: John Murray, 1850.

Traer, Robert. "Buddhist Affirmations of Human Rights." *Buddhist-Christian Studies* 8 (1988) 13–19.

Wijeyeratne, Eymard de Silva. "The Harvest Dream of Fr. Michael Rodrigo: Bread of Life for the People of Uva." *Sri Lanka Guardian*, May 14, 2010. http://www.srilankaguardian.org/2010/10/harvest-dream-of-fr-michael-rodrigo.html.

Woost, Michael D. "Developing a Nation of Villages: Rural Community as State Formation in Sri Lanka. *Critique of Anthropology* 14 (1994) 77–95.

Wright, Scott. "Reflection: Archbishop Oscar Romero—If They Kill Me, I Will Rise in the El Salvadoran People." Pax Christi USA, June 1, 2015. https://paxchristiusa.org/2015/06/01/reflection-archbishop-oscar-romero-if-they-kill-me-i-will-arise-in-the-salvadoran-people/.

www.ingramcontent.com/pod-product-compliance
Lightning Source LLC
Chambersburg PA
CBHW071509150426
43191CB00009B/1462